On 4th March 1987
Singapore
Declared Raffles Hotel A Historical Landmark
Under the Preservation of Monuments Board

Here are the legends, the stories, the events, which made this possible,
created and narrated by its former manager
Roberto Pregarz

Acknowledgements

The author wishes to express his heartful thanks to the following persons and companies for their valuable assistance, cooperation and information:

Raymond Flower
Ilsa Sharp
Andreas Augustin
Graham Byfield
Felix Zakariah
The Journalists and Writers
Raffles Hotel
Singapore Tourist Promotion Board
The Straits Times Group
National Archives
Preservation of Monuments Board
and the many others

First edition: 1990 Memories of Raffles
© Roberto Pregarz

New 2010 Raffles Legends and Stories
© Roberto Pregarz

ISBN: 978-981-08-4327-4

Produce by Nature Media Pte Ltd

Raffles
Legends and Stories

The Raffles Hotel, Singapore
Graham Byfield 1988

Roberto Pregarz

" Raffles is a living legend and legends have made Raffles one of the most famous hotels in the world"
(Painting by Graham Byfield)

Dedicated to
My Grandson Mikael

From Nonno

To An Old Friend

Raffles has always been unique, and doubtless it has emerged grander than ever after the reconstruction. Yet not so long ago it was in the doldrums regarded by many Singaporeans as an overrated colonial relic. There was even talk of pulling the hotel down.

The man who saved Raffles was Roberto Pregarz.

Arriving providentially in the early sixties. Roberto breathed new life into the place. With Italian flair and fervor he resuscitated old traditions and demonstrated conclusively how profitable nostalgia and history can be. Few visitors left Singapore without having a Singapore Sling in the Palm Court, or taking a memento of Raffles home with them.

Though anthropologists may speculate about the chemistry of a great hotel, they will agree that it owes its character to the personality of the man who runs it.

For Roberto, Raffles was a passion. He knew everything that was going on.

Steeped in its history, he was just as likely to be found up a ladder fixing decorations as in his managerial office, where the door was always open to writers and journalists, broadcasters and film directors. Indeed many of us soon became close personal friends.

Inspired by Roberto's enthusiasm, we have all written about Raffles, quoting the history and anecdotes that he told us. But now at last Roberto himself has put pen to paper in his own unique style, which someone described as 'neo-naive', droll, wistful, poignant, upbeat, and often hilariously funny, it is the voice of the man himself.

Roberto's achievements at Raffles have been recognized all over the world, not least by the Italian government which twice bestowed on him the proud title of Cavaliere - roughly the equivalent of a knighthood or the Legion d' Honneur. He is a prince of hoteliers, and I wish his charming memoirs of Raffles the success they deserve.

Raymond Flower

Valuable History

Managing Raffles Hotel, I have learnt how valuable HISTORY can be in promoting a hotel. It makes the hotel different, unique, famous and popular.

History is one of the major tourist attractions.

Travelers like to visit historical places which they have read of or have seen in movies or TV.

History is mainly related to a country, but I learnt that history can also be related to Hotels.

It does not need to be a Historical Hotel to find history.

- History can be linked to a hotel
- A hotel can make history
- History can be created around it.

and ....Then there are legends.

Who introduced me to Hotels and History was Raymond Flower.

Before he came to Raffles he wrote the book: "The Palace of St. Morritz". A hotel famous with personalities.

But his story was about St. Morritz with The Palace as centre stage. "The Old Ship" of Brighton, about the same.

History of Brighton around the Hotel.

Then came "Raffles, The Story of Singapore". The story of Singapore from Sir Stamford Raffles to Lee Kuan Yew.

Raffles Hotel again was in the limelight.

His last link between a place and a hotel was; "The Bayview and Penang".

His books and other writers made me appreciate how valuable history can be in the promotion of a hotel.

I managed 3 Hotels in Singapore. Each totally different from the other, but in all 3 I managed, I found a link to history which I developed and promoted.

Raffles everyone knows! But Cockpit? I developed its history linking it to the famous "Hotel de l'Europe"

Actually this hotel has a similar history to Raffles. It is a pity that was closed down in 1932. This famous name was used by the Cockpit but was changed to "Cockpit" when the new owner married a pilot.

The Crest of the Hotel was changed into... 2 fighting cocks! That was the end. Maybe one of these days, with the help of Raymond Flower I shall complete the writing of the history of "Hotel de l'Europe".

Then I managed River View. Modern, 500 rooms hotel.

I saw the potential value of it in the Singapore River and the Warehouses.

The Singapore River in 1991 was not what it is today. It was smelly and surrounded by dilapidated warehouses.

At that time I did not know that Lee Kuan Yew already had plans for the River.

I took over the Hotel in an original way.

I came on a tonkang accompanied by Raymond Flower and the Raffles barman who made the Singapore Sling on our journey up the river from the statue of Sir Stamford Raffles to the River View Hotel.

Is History valuable? Yes!

Roberto Pregarz

A Short History of Raffles Hotel

Raffles Hotel takes its name from Sir Stamford Raffles, the founder of Singapura, The Lion City.

lts history dates back to the early 1880s, beginning in a very small way as a *tiffin-house* within a private residence. During its initial stages, it was mainly concerned with serving luncheons, gradually developing into a kind of hostel. It was not until 1886 that Raffles Hotel actually came into being as one of a chain of hotels built by the Sarkies Brothers, three Armenian expert hoteliers who came to Singapore to seek fame and fortune.

The original building for the Hotel was a bungalow, situated at the corner of Beach Road and Bras Basah Road. It used to be the residence of a Captain and Mrs. Dare. In its early days, the Hotel had a fence along the frontage with the original entrance facing Bras Basah Road.

Beach Road, in those days, was the main residential area — the houses standing well back from the road with the gardens in front. One of the Chinese names for Beach Road is still known as the *Twenty-house Street*, deriving from a row of twenty elegant dwellings with large compounds belonging to the earliest straits merchants. It was said that most of these houses had a separate building for a billiard room and the annex of Raffles Hotel was one such room.

The sandy beach extended just beyond Beach Road and it was a common occurrence for the water to rise to the roadside. This is probably why Raffles Hotel has a few steps leading to the lobby. Eastward, beyond Beach Road, one and a quarter miles after the last European residence, was a Malay Village where the Sultan of Johore and his followers lived and where pirates used to congregate.

By the 1890s, the modest building proved to be inadequate to meet the demands of the growing port. With great faith, the Sarkies Brothers arranged for extensions to be added to the original bungalow and in 1896, on the 18th of November, Raffles was formally opened.

Behind the Hotel, there used to be stables for gharries, the conveyances that were used in those days. These were carriages drawn by one pony and led, not driven, by a groom with an occasional out-rider behind.

In the early 1900s, Raffles Hotel was one of the centres of social gaiety in Singapore and *The Savoy of Singapore* is the well-merited description given by the London Sphere to Raffles Hotel in 1905. Further testimony to the excellence of this palatial place of entertainment is borne in Rudyard Kipling's adivce, *Feed at Raffles when visiting Singapore* and in Senator Staniforth Smith's statement that *Raffles Hotel is more than a hostelry it is an institution — the hotel that has made Singapore famous to the tourists and an abode of pleasure to the residents.*

The world famous Singapore Gin Sling was created by one of our barmen in the famous Long Bar and was served in the Cads' Alley which later was renamed Gin's Alley in honour of this popular drink.

When the world depression hit Singapore in the 1930s, many hotels were forced to close but Raffles Hotel was able to hold its head above water, maintain its reputation and retain its position as Singapore's leading hotel.

In 1941 when the Second World War broke out in Malaya, Singapore was one of the worst cities to suffer regular bombing day and night. On one occasion, two bombs landed at the rear of the hotel, killing an Indian porter.

The hotel management had perfected a satisfactory black-out for its large dance room and the orchestra continued to play nightly till midnight and the waiters at the hotel remained on duty until the last moment.

When the Japanese invaded Singapore, the lobby of Raffles Hotel was filled with refugees while most of the staff fled with their families for safety. Singapore surrendered on 15th February, 1942 and, between that year and 1945, high ranking Japanese Officers took over the hotel. It was then that the main entrance was shifted from the front of the building to the corner of the Palm Court.

After the liberation on 12th September, 1945, Raffles Hotel became a hive of activity but in a very different way from that of the pre-war days. Instead of being a rendezvous of a cosmopolitan and wealthy selection of people it gave temporary shelter to hundreds of ragged refugees rescued from internment camps in Java and other islands of the East Indies. In the year 1946, Raffles Hotel reopened her doors to the public again.

1. ARSHAK SARKIES.   2. AVIET SARKIES.   3. TIGRAN SARKIES.

Today, Raffles Hotel has 104 suites, distinctively and elegantly furnished. The lofty ceilings and spaciousness of the rooms, two features rarely found in most modern hotel accommodation, are part of the old-world charm of Raffles Hotel and this attraction drew guests like Somerset Maugham to return again and again.

Raffles Hotel, built in the French Renaissance style is an architectural rarity. It occupies an area of over 200,000 square feet, set among tall, fanlike travellers palms and commands a panoramic view of a multi-racial city. From the breezy verandah one can watch the busy flow of the traffic below, the harbour ahead teeming with freighters and ships from all over the world and, within a stone's throw, the older part of Singapore town built around the Singapore River.

The hotel can indeed boast of a rich and colourful history with a wealth of stories and anecdotes woven around it. An old waiter of the hotel fondly recollected a certain Dutch anthropologist who used to consume eight to ten bottles of gin for breakfast every morning. Then there is the legend of a tiger being shot under the billiard table of Raffles Hotel by Mr. C. M. Phillips, the headmaster of Raffles Institution which was just across the road. In 1986 the legend roared back to life when Seta the tiger from the Chipperfield circus roamed the billiard room again.

Several personalities have stayed here: Robert Kennedy, Ava Gardner, Elizabeth Taylor, Princess Soraya and many others. Somerset Maugham, Rudyard Kipling, James Michener, Andre Malraux, Herman Hesse, Ilsa Sharp, Raymond Flower, Andreas Augustin.... wrote about Raffles.

Films: *Pretty Polly, Passion Flower* and TV series *Tenko, Tanamera and Hawaii Five-O* were also filmed in the Hotel.

Today, Raffles Hotel stands as a historic landmark, a living monument to Sir Stamford Raffles' energy and imagination. By virtue of its association with the historical past and Singapore's strategic geographical location, it is both a rendezvous as well as a place of transit for world personalities and leaders of the business world. Raffles Hotel is, for many travellers, a home from home. It is here that much of Somerset Maugham's Exotic East lingers on and to stay at Raffles Hotel is truly to enjoy the rare pleasure of tropical living at its finest.

"Raffles stands for all the fables of the Exotic East"

Somerset Maugham

Contents

Contents

Waiter! There Is A Tiger Under The Billiard Table

The Tiffin Room at Raffles is probably the most famous dining room in the world, not because of the personalities, beautiful women, heads of state and royalty who have banqueted there but because of the tigers.

The first tiger wandered inside Raffles Tiffin House some time in 1912 and was shot dead under the billiard room by the principal of the Raffles Institution. The second one however was more lucky.

There was nothing unusual on the 25th of January 1986.

I was watching the news at 9.00 pm when my son Andrea all excited told me, "Look papa, a circus is coming to town. Can you take us? "Yes, yes" I said by reflex.

At about 3.00 am that night I woke up with thoughts churning in my head.

A circus coming to town? There must be some tigers. Raffles is starting the centenary activities.

...The tale of the tiger shot under the billiard table...

Raymond Flower, a few weeks earlier, had launched the book *"Year of the Tiger, The Raffles Centenary"*.

In a few days the Chinese will be celebrating the New Year which will be the Year of the Tiger.

Click! ... All the things came together!

I jumped out of bed all excited! My wife thought I had a nightmare ... I said:

"I must get a tiger to Raffles as a highlight for the centenary celebrations." This is how it all began.

At that hour, I did not know how difficult it would be to get a tiger into the alcove of the Tiffin Room where our billiard table was. "Well," I said "it is an opportunity which I would not like to miss. Now, how to go about it? First, I have to find the tiger. Second, I have to find out whether it would be allowed to come to Raffles. Third, and most important, was how to get it to Raffles?"

The first thing in the morning, I drove to see Mr. Chipperfield, the owner of the circus, which was featured on the TV news.

He found my request quite unusual. However, after a short meditation he said, "Yes."

I almost kissed him, I was too happy. Having made a first step, I felt like Armstrong on the moon.

After the first excitement, however, I started to have second thoughts. Maybe this was not such a good idea. It would be a great risk. The hotel was full of guests, the tiger might escape and devour one of them. I was sure my Chairman would say "No" (knowing how conservative he was!) and think that I had gone crazy.

Should I ask him? Should I not?

What would I do if I were in his position? ... I would say "No!"

So I decided not to ask him.

What next now?

I had to check to which authorities I had to write to for permission so I asked Mr. Chipperfield for help. Was it the Ministry of Health? The Police? Parks and Recreation? Environment? Customs?

Here I started to receive the first set back. Every reply was "NO!" Should I give up? No, I then went to see a higher ranking officer.

My argument was that the Centenary of Raffles was only once in a 100 years and the year of the tiger only once in 12 years. To have them coincide was something very special.

Finally, most reluctantly, one by one they started to give me their permission. One week before Chinese New Year I had all the permits except for the one which was the most important: The Police! They refused to budge. It was a threat to the public they said. I insisted, I pleaded. They told me, "Come back tomorrow, tomorrow....."

Days passed, the New Year was approaching, 4th February (I almost forgot my birthday), 5th, 6th went to see the Chief of the Police. "Sorry, I am busy," he said, "I have a murder to deal with, come back later." I came back later. He wasn't in. I waited, six hours passed, finally he returned. Maybe out of frustration he said, "Yes! You have the licence." He signed it. But ... on the following conditions:

(1) Take up an insurance for S$1 million.
(2) Engage 8 police officers with guns.
(3) Build a cage around the billiard room.
(4) Don't advertise.
(5) Don't allow the public inside the Tiffin Room.

However he allowed the reporters, the press photographers, TV crew (only 100 of them in all to be there). It was not going to be an easy job to make preparations in the Tiffin Room without making the guests wonder why it was being closed.

My biggest worry actually was my Chairman. What would happen if he came for lunch and asked me why the Tiffin Room was closed and what was happening?

    8th February 1986

    Eve of the Year of the Tiger

    12.00 noon

A van drove in from the Bras Basah Road entrance of the Hotel and stopped in front of the billiard room. The door opened and three gentlemen wearing topees, came out with a tiger on the leash, and entered the billiard room.

The Tiffin Room was deserted. They had come earlier to enjoy a game of snooker while the tiger was getting acquainted with its surroundings. "Seta" was her name, (in Italian it means silk) for her fur gleamed like silk. She was a beautiful Bengali tiger, 1 1/2 years old weighing over 250 lbs. She enjoyed sniffing around the plants. She broke a Singapore Sling glass, for she too wanted to try the famous Gin Sling. She "blessed" some plants, and she chased the balls on the billiard table.

It was a great scene. I thought I was dreaming.

At about 2.00 pm, the reporters, the photographers and the TV crews started to come in. From that moment, cameras, videos and pens did not stop clicking, whirring nor scribbling - no, not even for a second. A gentleman who was temporarily assigned to SBC-TV kept up his Englishman's reputation acting as in Noel Cowards "Mad dogs and Englishmen" ... to its highest.

The Straits Times on Tuesday, February 11, 1986.

He went inside the billiard room to film the tiger while she was roaming about freely.

By 4 p.m. the tiger had extended her stay and our license had expired. It was time for me to present Mr. Chipperfield with a certificate to commemorate this great event and to thank him for having made the 100th anniversary of Raffles a most memorable one.
"Unfortunately" he refused to take the certificate through the bars. He wanted me to present it to him inside the billiard room, beside the tiger.
Well this gave me the paralyzing shock of my life. Mr. Chipperfield did not know that I was scared of dogs and that my Siamese cat had once, during a less affectionate mood, sent me to hospital to get 20 stitches on my leg.
The press, unfortunately for me, strongly supported Mr. Chipperfield's request and my personal doctor gave me a friendly and encouraging smile.
I went inside. I smiled. I shivered. But I did it! I presented the certificate not to Mr. Chipperfield but to "Seta", the tiger, who sniffed my hand in appreciation.
As soon as I could, I sneaked out. My wife, Helena, was braver, for she posed with Seta and caressed her.
I never thought that being the manager of a hotel would lead to such risks.
Luckily the 100th anniversary of Raffles comes once only in a life time.
By the way, my Chairman later confirmed that he would not have given his permission, but he thought that ... "it wasn't a bad idea".

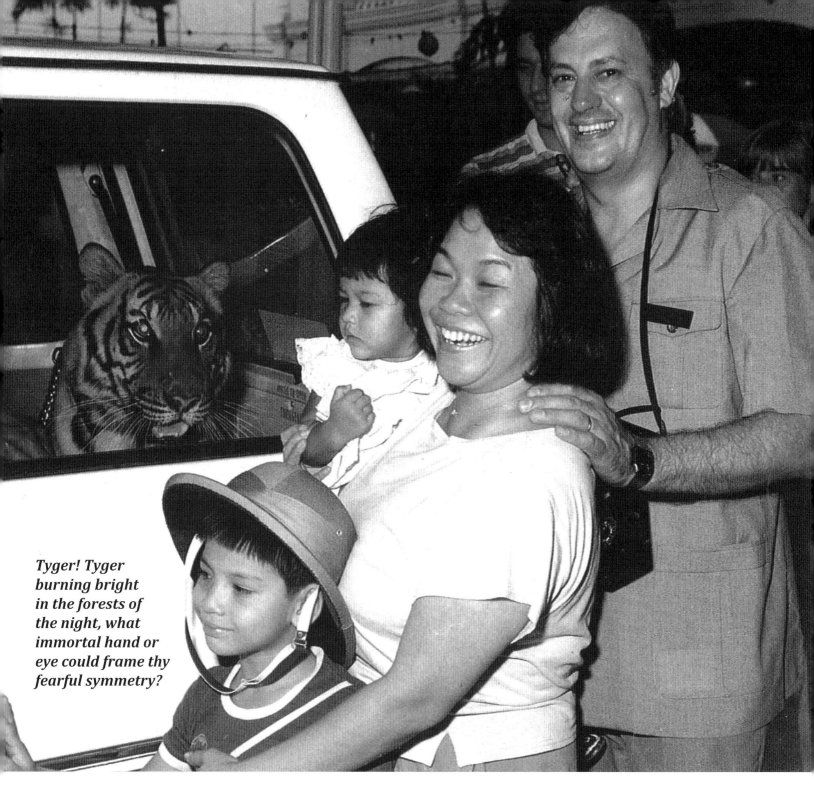

Tyger! Tyger burning bright in the forests of the night, what immortal hand or eye could frame thy fearful symmetry?

The Pregarz's family waves goodbye to Seta

16

Back in 1857 the tigers must have been enjoying life tremendously for they were tucking into a man-sized meal at the rate of 300 a year.

In 1887 the Government offered rewards to anybody catching a tiger which cheered the population no end and some very enthusiastic bouts of tiger shooting developed, including a group called 'The Tiger Club.'

There are still tigers in Johore just accross the causeway in Malaysia - and remember that tigers can swim that distance very easily!

. . . In 1998

British circus trainer mauled by tiger.

A British animal trainer with the Ringling Bros and Barnum & Bailey Circus was in critical condition on Wednesday after being mauled by a tiger.

Richard Chipperfield was undergoing surgery at Bayfront Medical Centre for severe trauma to the head, hospital spokesman Rob Summer Said.

Chipperfield, 24, was attacked by a 158-kg Bengal tiger on Wednesday morning.

Was it Seta?

Oh Coward! Oh Calcutta! Oh Raffles!

In July 1972 my Chairman called me. "Roberto, you take a holiday and when you come back you will take over Raffles".

"Mr. Chairman, I don't think I am prepared".

"I think you are. I'll help you."

During my holiday in London, I went to enjoy all the spots to savour and to learn about British culture, in anticipation of becoming the Manager of the famed British Raffles.

I went to the pubs, to the museums, to the library and to Noel Coward's shows.

Actually, when I met Sir Noel Coward at Raffles in 1968, I did not appreciate his fiddling on the piano in the corner of the Tiffin Room. He looked odd to me. But in London it was different. I enjoyed his musicals and I bought all his records.

As a finale of my holiday, I wanted to take a break from this "Oh" so British tour and enjoyed myself as a real tourist. So my wife and I went to see "Oh Calcutta".

Helena doing a painting of Noel Coward

Having been to other shows, we thought that to dress well was the code for every theatre. I put on my best suit and my wife wore a lovely long cheongsan.

Well, it was quite a change from the "Oh Coward" show we saw the previous night. Nothing in common except the "Oh". Yes it was "Oh, Oh, Oh" and some more "Oh". At the end of the first part, suddenly the London Bobbies burst into the theatre warning everybody that they were under house arrest for watching an obscene strip show.

Obviously the first two to be picked up were me and my wife. Dressed as we were and sitting in the front row? Quite embarrassing!

"Who are you?" . . . "Give me your names?" . . . "Where do you come from?"

My wife pinched me; "Say Raffles!"

Usually Italian men pinch and not get pinched. "Keep quiet!" I said, "if my Chairman comes to know that I have been watching an obscene show he will never give me the job as a Manager".

My wife said it was a joke. I thought it was too. But looking around I started to worry as the policeman did look real.

Better don't take risks.

It was a joke.

The audience clapped when they were told that I would be the next Manager of Raffles!

It was then that I realized how famous Raffles was.

When I returned from my holiday my predecessor wished me good luck and said, "Pity Raffles will close in 6 months!" So poor was the business and so rife were the rumors of the hotel being closed or pulled down. It didn't matter. I thought I'd be the youngest and shortest-lived Manager of Raffles, but still it would be my greatest honour.

However, I had to try my best. I listened to the advice of some of my good friends - Wallace Crouch, Dennis Pile, Morgan Lawrence and John Kilroy. "Roberto", they all said, "Raffles is famous - it has a lot of history. Visitors come from all over the world to see Raffles. Raffles is different. It's not an ordinary hotel."

At that time Raffles was not very much appreciated in Singapore. It carried the wrong image, a symbol of the past colonialism. The travel agents thought that it was too old and preferred the new Hilton-type.

I started to collect information about the history of the hotel and passed it to the visiting overseas journalists. They loved it! They published it and tourists started to return to Raffles.

One of the first things I did when I became Manager was to change the position of my desk and the location of the main bar.

> Feng Shui (Chinese geomancy)?
> Business acumen?
> A bit of both!
> It helped!

Before, the main bar was located far away from the lobby. Less than 20 Singapore Slings were sold each day. What to do?

> I shifted the bar nearer to the lobby (Later I discovered that this was the original location).
> I changed the name of the bar to "Long Bar".
> I built a longer bar counter.
> I put up the following signboard:

"Where the Singapore Sling originated"

The business grew, and grew and grew.

After this I looked at our Dining Room. The name, "Main Dining Room" had to be changed. But to what? The "Tiffin Room". Obviously, because Raffles started as a Tiffin House. This name gave me the opportunity to develop and promote the tiffin curry. I personally enjoyed the hot curries of Gomez, or the vegetarian curry at Komala Vilas or the Northern Indian of Omar Khayam but most of the tourists didn't. Visiting the East for the first time, they prefer the mild, spicy, tasty, not so-hot Raffles tiffin curry, and our Hainanese cooks were the experts on this.

Quite often the guests would ask me if I could give them a bit of our curry powder. I did, and when the demand increased, I decided to ask one of the manufacturers to mix spices as we did at Raffles and to make a souvenir package for sale. It was a great success. We even exported our curry powder to Japan and to Australia.

> TV crews filmed our tiffin curry and chef Ah Hong.
> The San Diego Philharmonic Orchestra organized a tiffin curry dinner to raise funds.
> Chef Chuang was flown to London to prepare tiffin curry for a Singapore promotion at Dickens and Jones.

And in 1978, H.R.H. Princess Sonia of Norway specifically requested to have a tiffin curry at Raffles and to meet the chef during her visit to Singapore.

For
Roberto Pregarz
A souvenir of
Noël.

THE STAGE CLUB, SINGAPORE

PRESENTS

AN EVENING WITH NOEL COWARD

AT THE

RAFFLES HOTEL

NOV. 25–27 and DEC. 1 & 2 at 8.30 P.M.

ARRANGED AND PRODUCED

by

SALLY TUNNICLIFFE

'Mad Dogs and Englishmen'

In tropical climes there are certain times of day
When all the citizens retire
To tear their clothes off and perspire.
It's one of the rules that the greatest fools obey,
Because the sun is much too sultry
And one must avoid its ultry-violet ray.
The natives grieve when the white men leave
    their huts,
Because they're obviously, definitely nuts!
Mad dogs and Englishmen
Go out in the midday sun,
The Japanese don't care to,
The Chinese wouldn't dare to,
Hindus and Argentines sleep firmly from twelve
    to one
But Englishmen detest a siesta.
In the Philippines
There arre lovely screens
To protect you from the glare.
In the Malay States
There are hats like plates
Which the Britishers won't wear.
At twelve noon
The natives swoon
And no further work is done,
But mad dogs and Englishmen
Go out in the midday sun.

It's such a surprise for the Eastern eyes to see,
That though the English are effete,
They're quite impervious to heat,
When the white man rides every native hides
    in glee,
Because the simple creatures hope he
Will impale his solar topee on a tree.
It seems such a shame
When the English claim
The earth,
They give rise to such hilarity and mirth.

Mad dogs and Englishmen
Go out in the midday sun.
The toughest Burmese bandit
Can never understand it.
In Rangoon the heat of noon
Is just what the natives shun,
They put their Scotch or Rye down;
And lie down.
In a jungle town
Where the sun beats down
To the rage of man and beast
The English garb
Of the English sahib
Merely gets a bit more creased.
In Bangkok
At twelve o'clock
They foam at the mouth and run,
But mad dogs and Englishmen
Go out in the midday sun.

Mad dogs and Englishmen
Go out in the midday sun.
The smallest Malay rabbit
Deplores this stupid habit.
In Hong Kong
They strike a gong
And fire off a noonday gun,
To reprimand each inmate
Who's late.
In the mangrove swamps
Where the python romps
There is peace from twelve till two.
Even caribous
Lie around and snooze,
For there's nothing else to do.
In Bengal
To move at all
Is seldom if ever done,
But mad dogs and Englishmen
Go out in the midday sun.

Andrea, And His Very Special Guests

Raffles became home for me and for my Singaporean-Chinese-Nonya wife and the staff was part of my family. Birthdays, weddings, funerals, we shared them all! Only in 1980, 10 years after our wedding, we were blessed with a child, a boy Andrea. Well he was not only our son but also the son of Raffles Hotel's staff. No royalty, no celebrity received greater attention than he. He was truly spoilt.

Well, we too spoilt him. After 10 years you tend to do so. When he started to walk, he spent most of the time going around the hotel with the maids, later on his own, but the watchful eyes of the staff were always behind him to protect him from any danger or mischief. Andrea knew every single employee by name. I didn't. He conversed in Mandarin with all the Chinese staff. I couldn't. He was allowed to do anything. I wasn't.

When he was four years old, he went to the Marymount Kindergarten. And here he gave me one of my biggest headaches. One day he told me, "Papa, my teacher wants to bring us to a special place during the holidays. I suggested to her to bring us to Raffles!" "What?" The next morning, the principal, Mrs. Shelley rang me and asked me whether it was all right for 40 "four-year-old" kindergarten children to visit Raffles. Can I say "no" to my son? No. I was used to taking heads of states, journalists and celebrities on tour of the hotel, but "four year-old kids? It was one of my biggest challenges! I had to organize something special. What would the kids like?

So I read my son's story books to get inspired.

When the day came, this was what they did.

> Visited the Somerset Maugham suite and talked about "ghosts".
> Had the Singapore "Kid" Sling at the Long bar.
> Danced the ronggeng and the lion dance on stage.
> Held a fishing competition in the Tiffin Room fountain.
> Ate gingerbread specially baked in the hotel kitchen.
> Made their own ice cream sundaes.
> At last, as a bonus I told the kids the story of the tiger at the billiard table.

The kids enjoyed the visit. And I did too!

Until the next day when I had another phone call.

"Mr. Pregarz" Mrs. Shelley again. "The afternoon session heard that the morning session kids had a wonderful time at Raffles. Can you do the same for another 50 kids?"

Thank you Andrea! - You are the greatest P.R.!

With Bruce Boxleitner

With Donnie and Marie

The children enjoying the show ...

Wartime Stories

The Man Who Stole The Spoon

Not often do you have a thief returning stolen property, but at Raffles it happened, and more than once too.

One day, my secretary, Mrs. Wee, left the following message on my desk. "The man who stole a spoon to eat his food in 1942 would like to see you." This 'thief' was a very special one. Mr. Harold Payne was in Changi Prison during the war and before being interned he took a spoon from Raffles. He used it for the next 3 1/2 years. His only possession.

He returned to Singapore in 1987 as President of the ex-prisoners of war for a reunion at Raffles, together with H.R.H the Duke of Kent and the foreign secretary Mr. Haseltine, who, unfortunately, was on his last official mission since he was sacked by Mrs. Thatcher upon his return.

After the official reunion ceremony Mr. Payne wanted to present to me his spoon as he knew of my effort to collect historical material for Raffles. It was a great, meaningful historical gift. I wanted to grab it. But I thought "Yes, it is of a great value to Raffles. But it is so much greater value to him." So I took a picture of the spoon and returned it to him.

The silver teaspoon; of great value for us at Raffles but of much greater value to Mr. Payne.

Raffles Revisited

Among the many persons who made return pilgrimages to Raffles was a lady who made a most unusual request. She wanted to see the bathroom of Room 73. The problem was that we did not have Room 73 anymore because the rooms had been renumbered according to the floor.

However, I managed to trace Room 73 to the present 116. Nothing unusual about this bathroom, large, yes, a bit damp, three steps down, old bathtub. What's so special then?

This lady stepped inside and tears filled her eyes. I left her alone.

Later she explained to me that her brother had often told her that the most memorable and exhilarating experience in his life was when he was released from prison in Changi during the Second World War, and had a bath, even without hot water, at Raffles. And he had it in this room.

```
In 1937    A Sailor, one of our guests, stole a glass bottom Malayan pewter tanker from the
           Long Bar.
           This gave him a sense of guilt and sleepless nights.
           For 7 years he sailed around the world and in every Port of Call, he engraved the
           name of the most popular pubs on the pewter tanker.
In 1946    He returned the pewter tanker to the Manager of Raffles Hotel
```

Raffles Never Again! Until...

One day a distinguished gentleman stood in the lobby, looking around, for quite some time.

I saw him because my office was just opposite. I decided to approach him and asked if I could be of any help.

He looked at me, "You must be Roberto Pregarz."

"Yes," I said, "How do you know?"

"I saw your photo in an Australian magazine and read several articles about you and Raffles. This is why I decided to return."

I wondered.

"Would you like to have a Singapore Sling with me at the Long Bar?" I asked

him. "Yes," he said, "with pleasure." Sipping the Singapore Sling he told me why he returned.

"In 1945, I was one of the first Australian soldiers to return to Singapore. I had been fighting in the jungles of Burma, Philippines and Borneo. I was just a corporal. When I was in school I read some Somerset Maugham novels which I enjoyed very much. So on the first day of my leave, I decided to visit Raffles.

As I entered Raffles, I felt exhilarated with the atmosphere; I could see Somerset Maugham, sitting in a corner of the Palm Court. I wandered among the majestic pillars, the long corridors, the Palm Court. I sat down too in a corner of the Palm Court. An old waiter approached me and asked me if I wanted a drink. "Yes," I said, "but also something to eat. What do you have?"

"Sorry," he said, "these days we only have bangers and mash."

"Oh, that would do perfectly for me". Wonderful to be at Raffles, the food was irrelevant after three years in the jungle. After few minutes, a gentleman in a coat approached me again.

"Are you of the rank of a lieutenant or higher?"

"No Sir" I replied, "I am a corporal and a devotee of Somerset Maugham."

"Sorry you must leave" he said.

"Gosh (I can't use the right word) Peace has broken out, I said. I left and swore that I would never step into Raffles again!

I must tell you that you had made me change my mind. I read about you, an Italian, and how - I quote from the newspapers - you have "restored the legend of the British Empire"

So here I am! Thank you for making me feel welcomed at Raffles.

Doris Geddes, Elizabeth Taylor, Malcom Forbes
A Strange Connection

Liz Taylor: The Geddes - Taylor story is another legend of Raffles

Among the tenants of Raffles, Doris Geddes was the Number One in many ways. She was a very enterprising Australian lady, and, in her younger days she must have been quite beautiful too. She was a talented pianist, a fashion designer and married one of the most eligible bachelors of one of the most prominent British families. At Raffles, she had the best boutique in town. My first encounter with her was through Wimpy, her cute little cocker spaniel.

One day, I saw Wimpy "blessing" one of the pillars along the corridor and I chased him away. A few minutes later Doris Geddes burst into the Manager's office and complained about me. I had to apologise to her. The next day, Miss Geddes called me to her office and mixed her own special dry Martini for me.

This became a regular affair for the next 15 years. A love-hate affair. One day she would come with her lawyer threatening to take me to court (due to no fault of mine), and the next day she would mix another dry martini for me.

Once she gave an interview to a popular weekly magazine. She must not have been in the right mood with me that day as the newspaper quoted her as saying that the Manager of Raffles who was a "jumped up waiter" was spoiling her business and reputation.

But when this was published, she was in a good mood with me, rushed to my office and apologised to me. "For what?" I said. "For insulting you!" she said.

"Oh, I thought it was a compliment," I replied.

Between one dry martini and another, Doris Geddes was very talkative.

She talked about her younger days (she was then in her 70s), about the charitable tea dances and fashion shows she used to organize in the Raffles Ballroom, about her beautiful European models some of whom were wives of very prominent people, and about Elizabeth Taylor. After H.R.H. the Sultana of Johore, for whom she designed a wedding gown, Elizabeth Taylor must have been her second most valuable client.

At that time Miss Taylor came with Mike Todd and bought a dress. Doris Geddes told her that it was a bit too small for her but Miss Taylor insisted. Later that day, in the middle of the dinner given in Miss Taylor's honour, the zip gave way and a good portion of Elizabeth's body became exposed to the pleasure of the male diners.

This is a well known story, but unfortunately I could not verify it with Miss Taylor when she came back with Mr. Malcolm Forbes. During his visit to Singapore, Mr. Forbes wanted to fly a giant balloon in the shape of an elephant, from the Padang. Maybe he wanted to land at Raffles. For sure he wanted to visit the hotel and I was informed of his imminent arrival.

What shall I do, I thought, to welcome such a personality with such unusual hobby. Making a special Singapore Sling would be just too ordinary. So I decided to borrow a trishaw from one of the trishaw riders outside the hotel and gave him a ride inside Raffles.

I was pedalling and telling the history of Raffles while Mr. Forbes was enjoying his Singapore Sling and the ride on the trishaw. He was so happy that he invited me to have a ride in his balloon.

I was thrilled, honoured, but scared to death just thinking about THAT RIDE!

Luckily the police did not allow him to fly his balloon.

From his balloons to a trishaw ride!

To Cav. Pregany Roberto
It's wonderful to again – be a well part of the fabulous "Raffles" tradition, to – again – enjoy their unique hospitality –

Malcolm Forbes

May 3, 1985

Somerset Maugham, Another Story

"Raffles stands for all the fables of the exotic east!"
This is what Somerset Maugham said about Raffles during a casual conversation with Franz Schutzman (manager of Raffles in the l950s). This most brilliant and most colourful hotelier made sure that this casual statement would become the motto and well-merited description for Raffles, even though Somerset Maugham was not really appreciated by the British community in Singapore nor welcomed at the Tanglin Club.

Somerset Maugham was right, so was Franz Schutzman. Raffles really was famous and stood for "all the fables of the exotic east"

Raffles became famous not only in Europe and in the United States but throughout the west and also Japan. During the past few years the Somerset Maugham suite was occupied, mainly by young Japanese couples or young Japanese ladies. No one Japanese journalist, photographer or TV crew missed this famous suite. The Japanese love British tradition.

Why was it so special?

Of course, Somerset Maugham stayed there during his last visit in 1959-1960. There also was a nice old fashioned wicker rattan settee and a very large four-posters brass bed where, on one occasion, 10 travel agents lay on the bed side by side and took a picture.

Hundreds of stories have been written about Somerset Maugham and Raffles.

One day, Wendy Hutton, a popular travel writer came to see me and asked me. "Roberto. I have written so many stories about Somerset Maugham and my editor still wants another one. Can you help me? I don't know what to write."

I had just finished reading a story in The Straits Times about the connection between Somerset Maugharn stories and the real events that inspired him. This was about the story, "The Letter", which Somerset Maugham wrote ten years after The Straits Times reported that Mrs. Proudlock was convicted of killing her lover.

In "The Letter" Mrs. Proudlock's name was changed to Mrs. Joyce.

Mrs. Proudlock was particularly famous for entertaining her guests with the Million-Dollar Cocktail which she had created. What happened was that after the trial the Million — Dollar Cocktail became the most famous drink in Singapore and Malaya and was served in every bar and at every party. But it survived only at Raffles because the Ngiam bartenders carried on the tradition from generation to generation.

Well, let's go back to Wendy's request.

Recipe of the Million Dollar Cocktail
Beefeater Gin,
Sweet & Dry Vermouth,
Egg White,
Pineapple Juice,
Angostura Bitter

"O.K.   Wendy I think I have an idea for you how you can find some inspiration. Tonight you'll stay in the Somerset Maugham suite. Just yourself. But before you go to bed, I shall set up a table for two in the sitting room, and Ho Wee How, who used to be Somerset Maugham's room boy, will serve dinner for two, for you and Mr. Somerset Maugham. I know from Ho what Somerset Maugham liked to eat. He will also serve the Million-Dollar Cocktail, a bottle of Chateau St. Emilion and a Scotch and water just before you go to bed,"

"Wonderful," She said, "I'll come back tonight."

I had a good idea in my mind, and wanted to keep it as a secret.

I quickly wrote down a conversation based on "The Letter" between Somerset Maugham and Mrs. Joyce.

I then rushed to one of my oldest residents Mr. Berrill who was enjoying his first Scotch of day at the Long Bar and I quickly ordered another double.

I said, "Mr. Berrill, have a drink on me." He never refused. After the drink, I asked him whether he could do me a favour.

"I have to tell someone a story, but my English pronunciation is not so good. You know I am Italian so can you read it to me? I'll tape it .... Thank you Mr. Berrill".   He did it in a disembodied voice.

I rushed down to my office and I called a carpenter to meet me at the Somerset Maugham suite. There, we opened a panel of the ceiling above the bed and placed a tape recorder. Then we connected a wire to a switch outside the back of the room.

Wendy came back to the hotel at about 7.30 p.m. She was beautifully dressed. She wore a long white dress with a lot of frills, a white hat with a lot of flowers and she had a fan in her hand. She looked almost like Mrs. Joyce.

"Welcome Mrs. Joyce," I said, "Mr. Maugham is expecting you." And I accompanied her to the suite. "Have a nice evening"

"Good night"

I left her alone.

She enjoyed the cocktail, the dinner, the wine and the scotch. At about 11 .30 p.m. the lights went off. I waited until 1.30 a.m. then I switched on the tape recorder and adjusted the volume first to low and then to a bit louder. A disembodied voice resonated:

Hello my dear,
What are you doing in my room? Are you reading my "letter". The story you told me the first time I saw you, you had never varied in the smallest detail.
You told it as coolly then, a few hours after the tragedy, as you are telling it now. You told it connectedly, in a level, even voice, and your only sign of confusion was when a slight colour came into your cheeks as you described one or two of the incidents. You were the last woman to whom we would have expected such a thing to happen...

A light went on, I turned the volume to low again, then I turned it off. After half an hour, the light went off. I played the recorder again softly.

Your husband. Robert, had gone to Singapore for the night. Though alone, you had dressed for dinner in a tea—gown and afterwards worked at your lace in the sitting room ...

Then I turned it again a bit louder.

Hammond, your planter friend, had called unexpectedly having left his car some distance from the house. You had continued with your lace: Hammond had spoken of local affairs, the races in Singapore, the price of rubber and a tiger seen in the neighborhood.
Suddenly he had said. "I wish you wouldn't wear those great horn spectacles. I don t know why a pretty woman should do her best to look plain."
"Sweet of you, but I can only think you half-witted," you had replied,
When he declared his love for you. You had bade him goodnight and were about to call the houseboy when Hammond had seized and embraced you.
You had struggled but he had lifted you off your feet and dragged you to the bedroom. "A perfect savage".
Then he had stumbled. You had picked up a revolver (left there for your protection) and, frantic with terror, not quite knowing what you were doing, shot him. You had heard a cry, and seen him lurch out onto the verandah ...

Suddenly, not one but all the lights came from the bedroom, the dressing room, the sitting room and the bathroom.
I turned down the volume again.

You followed and emptied the revolver into him as he lay crumpled and bloody on the ground.
Later you had told your husband and the Assistant District Official.' "He tried to rape me, and I shot him " — a simple case and a simple response.
Good night Mrs. Joyce, sweet dreams.

The lights stayed on the whole night although I believe Wendy went to sleep at about 5.00 a.m.
At about 11.00 a.m. Wendy came to my office.
"Roberto," she said, "You wouldn't believe it, there was a real ghost in my room. It was wonderful. It was scary. I have a fantastic story."
"Oh, I am so happy," I said.
I kept quiet, I didn't want to spoil her dream ...

The Sunday Times feature story which inspired me.

Sir Winston Churchill, An Unusual Gift

Mr. S Darn-Kenth presents the painting to Roberto

Many visitors to the Writers Bar have admired the large painting of Sir Winston Churchill which was prominently displayed opposite that of Queen Elizabeth I. Did Sir Winston stay at Raffles? Did he mention Raffles? Looking at him always brought back memories of Singapore in 1942 when he made this announcement:
"Singapore is an impenetrable fortress! It will never fall!"
Bang! ... Bang! ... Bang!
Then 15 February 1 942.
The British surrendered.

Raffles had always an image of being discriminatory in the mind of Singaporeans until an Italian married a Singaporean and became manager of Raffles.
Ironically, this British institution had only been under British management for two years but over 40 under Italian.

The greatest compliment I ever received was the headline in an Australian newspaper: "A nostalgic Italian helps to restore a legend of the British Empire".

Well, this is a bit too much, although I did revive the British traditions and ensured, with the help of my wife, that Raffles was not to be regarded a symbol of the British colonialism, but as an abode of pleasure for the visitors as well as for the Singaporeans who came to dine or to stay.

But back to Sir Winston Churchill.

Mrs. Leon-Soh, who was the first lady parliamentarian in Singapore thought that the best location for the portrait of Sir Winston Churchill, which was painted by her close friend Keith Darn-Kenth, would be Raffles.

So with a simple ceremony, and a few speeches dedicated to the special relationship between Singapore and the United Kingdom, the portrait of Sir Winston Churchill, which was wrapped in the flags of Singapore and Great Britain, was handed over to me in appreciation for my small contribution to the preservation of a legend of the British Empire.

A Journey Into The Past, A Special Encounter

Tunku Abdul Rahman, the first Prime Minister of Malaysia, was quite shocked when he returned to Raffles on March 13, 1984. The first things he saw in front of the hotel were army trucks, British soldiers, sand bags and barbed wire.

He thought that his mind was playing tricks. He rubbed his eyes. A minute later, 80 Malay drummers welcomed him in the traditional way as he made his entrance into the Ballroom for a special Muslim function. As I accompanied him, he asked me, "What's happening down there?"

"Oh sorry for the mess." I said, "BBC is filming *Tenko*".

"Oh, can you tell me more about it later?"

This was another busy day for me.

At the front entrance the BBC was filming the 37 episodes TV series Tenko which in England upstaged Dallas. There were about 100 actors and crew.

The hotel was full too and I had to create another entrance and another reception for my guests, in order to allow filming in the proper location. The BBC is famous for its accuracy.

In the Ballroom, we had a tea reception for the Tunku and 400 Muslim community leaders. In the Tiffin Room we were making preparations for the wedding of the year between the children of two prominent Indian families. They had asked for a traditional Hindu wedding in a British setting with British food but without the roast beef and Yorkshire pudding.

In the Palm Court a Japanese crew was filming a popular Japanese singer for an international show.

At the end of the tea party, after a number of speeches, the Tunku or "Bapa Malaysia" (this has how affectionately he was known), called me to ask about the filming and about the history of Raffles Hotel. Among all his other interests he was also a writer and enjoyed history which he made. Actually, he talked more than I did. When I told him that I had a photo of him with Dato David Marshall having a meeting in the Elizabethan Grill, his eyes glittered.

Dato David Marshall and Tunku Abdul Rahman in the Elizabethan Grill

Roberto getting the Tunku to autograph the historic picture

"Oh, my friend Marshall, did you see him recently? How is he? Did he see this photo?"

"Yes," I said. "And he autographed it for me. Could you do the same?", "With pleasure!" he said.

A friendly encounter between a Jew and a Muslim! The British, the Indians and the Japanese all at once.

At Raffles, anything can happen!

Christmas At Raffles

Christmas at Raffles was always celebrated in the traditional style since the early 1930s. Actually I made it a point that, while the other hotels became more innovative, I had to continue this tradition in the most conservative way. The same menu, the same decorations, the same caroling.

However, sometimes we made it a bit different.

In 1986, during the 100th anniversary of Raffles Hotel, I engaged a hundred member caroling group from Peter Low. A few days later, one hundred prominent American businessmen and wives, all dressed in Santa Claus costume, rode in trishaws from Orchard Road to Raffles to have Singapore Slings.

In 1986, the TV stations of England, Singapore, Australia and New Zealand organized a live telecast of the Noel Edmond Show where the Prime Ministers of the respective countries exchanged Christmas greetings and messages of peace. The highlight of the programme however, was a secret reunion planned in each country by the TV stations for a special friend.

Mr. Parker, an Englishman, was invited to Raffles to watch and exchange greetings with his family in England through the live telecast. They were all there around the Christmas tree except for his younger brother.

Suddenly the telecast in the Tiffin Room was almost interrupted by two lions prancing just behind Mr. Parker. This was a special Singapore greeting for London viewers to get a feeling of Christmas in Singapore. When the drums and cymbals subsided, the London reporter asked Mr. Parker what was his Christmas wish. Mr. Parker replied, "To be with someone from my family."

"Turn around," the reporter said.

"What?" Mr. Parker turned and saw two lions and hundreds of people. Suddenly somebody jumped out of the lion's costume. It was his brother! This was one of the most exciting Christmases.

Mr Parker and the lions on the SBC and BBC live telecast of the Noel Edmond Show in the Tiffin Room

I was lucky to have Michael Chang among my staff who was more than the restaurant manager. He was an artist and a sculptor! He made a styrofoam sculpture for every occasion.

A Chinese dragon for Tan Sri Tan Chin Tuan's special party.

A Merlion for the STPB.

A bunny for Easter.

A tiger for the billiard room.

And for Christmas a lot of reindeer and a Santa Claus.

That year he made a very special Santa Claus, eight feet tall, which we placed right in the lobby at the entrance of the Long Bar under the sign "Home of the Singapore Sling!"

That year we had an exceptionally prosperous Christmas. The hotel was packed every day.

Yes, the U.S. Navy with its 10,000 sailors was in town. And Raffles was a place to visit for them too. Their parents had reminded them not to miss Raffles when in Singapore and they didn't. These navy boys often got into trouble, but never at Raffles! They came for a Singapore Sling and most had more than one.

Almost each one of them took a picture with Santa Claus in front of the Long Bar. This was a very special souvenir for them.

One morning Michael Chang rushed to my office hopping mad. "Mr. Pregarz, you can't believe it, my Santa Claus has disappeared right under the nose of the receptionists! You should fire them, they must have been sleeping last night!"

I made enquires ... No one saw, no one heard, no one could explain how an eight feet tall Santa Claus could have suddenly disappeared.

The next day I received a trunk call. "This is the Captain of the U.S.S. Saratoga. I must apologize to you on behalf of the U.S. navy. We found a Santa Claus in the crew's recreation room. When we asked who made it, they told me that they stole it from Raffles. While a few of the sailors kept your receptionists busy, the others took the Santa Claus over the fence, got onto a trishaw and brought it on board just before we sailed. They will be severely punished. Please let me know how much it costs. We'll send you double the amount with our official apologies."

"Don't worry Captain," I said, "I was a sailor too. And I am honoured that our Santa Claus has made it a special Christmas for your boys! Please keep it, and Merry Christmas from the Staff of Raffles!"

Helena and Elisabetta with some of the 100 Santas and Santarinas

Mr. Ho, His Birds And An Unhappy Guest

Raffles' staff were not just ordinary staff.
- Some were athletic champions, like Kamal.
- Some were artists, like Judy Chia and Michael Chang.
- Some used to model, like Rita.
- Some were great mahjong players, who more than once had to be interrupted to serve dinner to the guests.
- Some had special hobbies.
Mr. Ho's hobby was to train the singing birds.
When he was in Malaysia he used to be the personal cook of a Malaysian Minister who loved singing birds.
He had over 100 of them in his large residence and Mr. Ho enjoyed listening to them as well as looking after them.

Eddie Rose

RAFFLES MORNING

Birds sing
A haunting song of the woods.
Palms fan --- boldly screening
Orchids running merrily
up tall spikes --- dripping colour
and the little sparrow
at my feet runs free and brown.
Frangipani blooms
like the beautiful women
by the pool --- as maidens of old
by the crater

Joy Beaudette Cripps

Chef Ho with one of his precious birds

When he came to Singapore, Mr. Ho missed these birds so, after getting his first salary, he bought one, then two, then three ... and then he had fifteen birds. In his HDB flat there was not much space left. Birds in the kitchen, birds in the bathroom, birds in the corridor, birds in the sitting room ...

One night he told his wife he saw a beautiful bird in the shop and ... his wife saw this bird ... coming into their bedroom! That day must have been a tough day for her, three teenage children, washing, cooking and the sixteenth bird ...!

She screamed!

"Either the birds go out of this house or I will go!" she shouted at the husband.

Mr. Ho is a very nice man. He showed consideration for his wife. The staff had a large open space at their quarters at Raffles, so he brought his birds there, and his colleagues too loved the birds. At the last count there were more than 40 of them, who found a home at Raffles.

One day we had to reserve the whole Tiffin Room for a special heritage exhibition to be opened by HE Mr. S Rajaratnam, Singapore's former Foreign Minister. I was in a dilemma where to serve breakfast for my guests. The other rooms were full too. The only alternative was the Palm Court.

It may be too hot, the guests might complain. I thought ...

That day, in Orchard Road there was a bird singing competition and this inspired me. I quickly called Mr. Ho and asked him to display all his singing birds in the Palm Court. We attached a label to each cage and made a description of each bird. Then I introduced this new attraction in the breakfast menu and wished my guests a pleasant day. It was a hit. Several poems and even a book were dedicated to our singing birds by our appreciative guests. The breakfast had moved permanently to the Palm Court until one day, ...

Mr. Ho as usual, that morning at 10.30 a.m, came to the Palm Court to take some of his most special birds to feed them, to bath them, and to give them a rest. Suddenly, an elderly lady jumped up screaming and rushed to him.

Mr. Ho that day come out in his full chef's uniform and with a large knife tucked in his belt.

The lady thought that he was going to ...

"These Chinese can cook anything!" she must have thought.

Raffles Writers

Raffles Hotel would not have survived without the writers, without the journalists. For they helped it to thrive. Wallace Crouch, from the Sydney Morning Herald, was the first journalist to help me when he stayed at Raffles, a few months after I took over as Manager.

My good friend Dennis Pile, who at that time was the director of STPB for Australia, introduced him to me. The hotel was almost empty, there was not much to do, so we had plenty of time to talk.

That time I listened carefully to Wally who told me what he knew about Raffles and the Australian connection. Later I told the stories to the journalists who came to interview me.

A few days later he published a story about Raffles in his newspaper. In addition, he made an appeal to his readers to send me information and memorabilia on Raffles. Letters came, more journalists visited the hotel and wrote about "Raffles." Menus and "souvenirs", such as sugar bowls which disappeared in 1903 to the total disappointment and displeasure of the Sarkies, were returned and personal photographs were sent to me.

Not every journalist was pleased with Raffles, as some articles they wrote were controversial, some derogatory, some sarcastic. But generally most were satisfied and wrote one thousand flattering articles.

Here are some of the most interesting headlines.

Raffles. Where Old Ways Survive by Jean Simmons
Raffles. An Elegant Aroma Of Age by Jerry Hulse
Waiter, There s A Tiger Under The Table
by John Smith
Raffles Reprieved, Old Citadel Of Colonial Asia Will Not Disappear by Wallace Crouch
Raffles Turns Back The Clock by Eric Page
Memories Of Intrigue Ensconced At Singapore's Raffles Hotel by Choral Pepper
Historic Landmark Going Concern by Ann Terrill
New Lease Of Life For Eastern Savov
by Geoffrey Weston
Sunset On The Empire But The Memory Lingers With A Gin Sling by Joseph Galloway
Old Haunts Of Mad Dogs And Englishmen
by James Murray
Raffles. Where The Ghosts Of Kipling And Maugham Sip Gin Slings by Graham Goodman
Raffles, An Institution That (Luckily) Refused To Die
by Stanton H. Party
Raffling Around In Old Singapore by Chris Barnet
Bogies Drawled "Schweetheart" Seems To Echo In Raffles by Ronald Yates
Raffles Hotel Never Let The Sun Set
by Joseph Galloway

How could I say thanks to them. No amount of money could pay for their articles, which had contributed to the business, the fame, the popularity of Raffles.

I used to meet them in the Grill Bar.

Grill? ... what a name.

Writers Bar is a more appropriate name!

So Raffles had a new name for its watering hole, the rendezvous for local and foreign correspondents who met and talked about their latest assignments in Vietnam, Cambodia, Burma, Philippines. Laos, China and Singapore.

The first event which took place in this Writers' Bar was a show in which selections from Somerset Maugham, Rudyard Kipling, Joseph Conrad and Noel Coward were read out, sung or dramatized by the newly formed Raffles Group under the leadership of Sally Tunnicliffe.

After this, I thought that Somerset Maugham, Rudyard Kipling, Joseph Conrad and Noel Coward deserved a bit more than just a photo in the Writers Bar. So I decided to name the suites around the Palm Court after them and also after other famous writers from the past and from the present, those who stayed at Raffles or wrote about the hotel.

- Noel Barber featured Raffles in his novel Tanamera
- Robert Elegant spent his honeymoon at Raffles
- James Michener complained to me that although Raffles was his second home, no one paid attention to him until he met me.
- Andre Malraux loved the salmon-colored Mussanda Dona Luz flowering shrubs at the Palm Court.
- While Rudyard Kipling (From Sea to Sea) was impressed with Raffles' food ... "Providence conducted me along the beach in full view of five miles of shipping, five solid miles of masts and funnels to a place called Raffles Hotel where the food is excellent. Let the traveler take note Feed at Raffles when in Singapore".
- Herman Hesses (Extract from his diary notes dated 25th October 1911 taken from Aus Indien) wasn't so happy. "I like Singapore better this time, we are staying expensively but well at Raffles Hotel".
- Gavin Young spent several months at Raffles writing "Slow Boat to China".
- Dennis Bloodworth launched "An Eye for the Dragon" at Raffles.
- Arthur Hailey looked at Raffles for new Roots.
- Maxine Hong Kingston loved 3 things: Publicity, Raffles and her Husband.
- Kelly Chopard wrote a story for children about the tiger at Raffles.

The President and the Members of the Foreign Correspondents Association having a drink at the billiard table before the arrival of the tiger.

Joseph Galloway, UPI Bureau Chief of Singapore who had his office at Raffles, send's warmest greetings from Moscow: "Raffles Gang - Wish you were all here."

The first book on Raffles came from lIsa Sharp after three years of extensive research.

"There is only one Raffles" was born.

The second and the third books came from Raymond Flower.

Raffles, "the story of Singapore" and "Year of the Tiger, The Centenary of Raffles". This title was changed to "Meet You at Raffles", in the subsequent edition.

Then came a series from Andreas Augustin. He has made Raffles his home in Asia from 1986 until the very night when the hotel was closed for renovations. Here he wrote his first book about Raffles "The Most Famous Hotels". He later created his Treasury series, starting with "The Raffles Treasury", which became another bestseller about the hotel. Credit to him must also go for the "discovery" of Raffles' original plans at the Singapore National Archives which had eluded me, the architects and other writers. And the last writer to whom a room was dedicated to was Russell Foreman whose book was called 221 Raffles as this was the number of his suite.

I think I should tell you how 221 Raffles came about.

Raymond Flower was a regular visitor to Raffles. He combined pleasure with his business of writing. He found inspiration at Raffles but had not much time for writing since most of the time, he was called up by Mrs. Vayloo, who was managing our souvenir shops, to autograph his books at Raffles Little Shop or at the Writers Bar. He duly obliged. In fact he not only autographed his hook, but made it a point to write a small dedication according to the interest of the person or to the special event for whom the book was bought.

I don't think there is any other book that has been autographed for so many leading heads of states and personalities as "Raffles, the Story of Singapore". To the Agha Khan, to the President of Italy, to the Archbishop of Canterbury and to Margaret Roberts!

Who was Margaret Roberts? She was a student at the Somerville College, Oxford in whose bathroom Raymond Flower had a bath. By tradition, every under-graduate at Oxford had to do something special. At that time, the women's colleges were strictly out of bounds to men.

This lady is now called Mrs. Margaret Thatcher — The Former British Prime Minister.

Raymond Flower's favourite period to come to Singapore had always been winter (in Europe) because he said the bill to heat his house (castle actually) in Chianti is almost the same as spending a holiday in Singapore. (He hates winter and loves Singapore and Raffles).

One day, I told him. "Now we have five hooks on the history of Raffles and a children's book. What about you writing a thriller?"

"Well Roberto," he said, "I am a historian, I don't know how to write such a book."

A week later he left for Australia and two weeks later he sent me a telex.

Dear Roberto,

I found a writer for your thriller! He is my friend Russell Foreman, the author of "Long Pig" which sold over 2 million copies and which has been translated into five languages.

He is going to England but has agreed to stop over in Singapore to discuss with you whether there is any material which could inspire him.

Two weeks later, Mr. Foreman arrived. We had dinner together. We had roast-beef from the silver wagon ... Wait ... I told him the story about the piece of silver. The next day he postponed his flight and wrote the first 50 pages of 221 Raffles.   ... About the search for a hidden treasure.

And somebody said that Raffles wasn't inspiring!

How were we inspired for the launching of his book? Mr. Foreman and I were in the billiard room trying to find out where his "famous treasure" could have been hidden. I saw a crack in the marble floor ...

The night before the launching of the book, we removed two cracked marble floor slabs in the billiard room, and we dug a hole, big enough for an old-sailors chest. The soil was sandy. Half way through we found an obstruction. We dug carefully, and found some old bricks. Later these were identified as part of the original foundation of Captain Dare's bungalow. When the hole was big enough we put the chest inside. We filled the latter up with copies of 221 Raffles, and covered the enclosed chest with sand. Next we placed some old silver from the Sarkies period and put the marble slabs back.

The next day, a few days before the closure of Raffles, the last treasure was unearthed.

*Raymond Flower, Russell Foreman, Shirley Hew and Roberto uncovering Raffles last "treasure" -- **221 Raffles***

Filming At Raffles

To watch films being made at Raffles was a wonderful experience. I truly enjoyed all the excitement in the same way as the producers and all the crew did. Besides, the films were a great promotional value to Raffles.

I personally took care because I wanted to make sure that Raffles had the best exposure.

When a Japanese crew planned a film in Singapore with some shots at Raffles, as usual I took them around the hotel to show them the most interesting spots.

At the end of the hour, they asked me whether I had worked at Cinecitta (Rome's Hollywood) before, and whether Jean Paul Belmondo was my brother?

I said "No" to both. "But thank you for the compliment." In the end, not only a few shots were made at Raffles, but the theme was based on Raffles and bore the title: Raffles Hotel.

Hayley Mills and Trevor Howard take a break from filming Pretty Polly

Many films and TV series were made at Raffles including Pretty Polly. Tenko, St. Jacques. No Room at Raffles, Passion Flower and others. They all had one thing in common: during each filming, the producer made everybody know that he was in charge of the hotel and not the Manager!

The worst and most boisterous crew was the one who filmed Hawaii Five 0. The lobby was like an electric power station with cables running all over. There were more policemen to protect Jack Lord than Henry Kissinger when he visited Raffles. The car park had been converted into a hawker centre for a stunt chase in a Rolls Royce at 80mph between the stalls, to pin the villain against a wall.

These scenes had been rehearsed more than 100 times and all the stall holders were professional stuntmen who had to jump like frogs when the Rolls Royce swung around them. Our real hawkers would have been stunned and died of a heart attack or knocked over with kway teow, mie goreng and rojak running down their faces.

The "Women behind the Wire"

Celebrating the end of BBC's 37 TV Series "Tenko"

A scene of Tanamera -- dinner and dance in the most famous dinning hall

The Film Producers

Many famous film producers came to Raffles. One of them was William Wyler, a quiet simple person and an admirer of Somerset Maugham.

He wanted to stay in the Somerset Maugham suite.

One of his films which I enjoyed most was *Ben Hur,* and when I told him this, he gave me an autographed photo of this famous movie.

Another was Milos Foreman. He too loved Raffles, in particular the Palm Court. For a press interview he bought a Palm Court T-shirt and gave the interview at the Palm Court. "For good luck," he said. A few weeks later he won the Oscar for Amadeus.

One of the most difficult film producers to deal with must have been Otto Preminger. Not for me this time, but for another film producer.

American Express had commissioned a producer to film Otto Preminger for their new motto: *Don't leave home without it!*

This must have been one of the rare times that Otto Preminger was in front of the camera instead of behind it. He gave a hard time to the producer and to the cameraman who was trying to film him paying the bill with the American Express Card after a candlelight dinner at the Palm Court. Otto Preminger shouted, scolded, went behind the camera to teach the producer what to do without realizing that making a commercial was quite different from making a Hollywood movie.

William Wyler gave an autographed picture of Ben Hur to Roberto Pregarz

Mozart in the Palm Court, anyone? Milos Foreman, director of Amadeus seems to think it a splendid idea

But the most controversial film producer for sure had to be Peter Bogdanovich, the producer of *St. Jacques.* When he came to Raffles he spent a lot of time talking to me about his film and the sentimental reason for producing it. We walked a lot around the hotel. He loved Raffles and he told me, "Roberto, I want Raffles at its best in my movie. It will be good for you". We worked harder for this.

The leading actor, Ben Gazzara too loved Raffles. And he was Italian - Sicilian - and there was no difference in his behaviour whether he was acting or relaxing. He was eloquent, exuberant and because I was Italian too we spent many hours talking at the Writers Bar, sharing our love for Sicily.

Sicily was his home, not mine. But I spent almost two years there during my national service. Although this region is well known for the mafia, its people are warm-hearted, friendly and honest Italians.

A few months later, I was shocked to read in the local newspaper that Peter Bogdanovich had cheated the Ministry of Culture and changed the script in order to film the most shady areas of Singapore.

Dear me, I said, what about Raffles? Nobody mentioned anything about Raffles in *St. Jacques*. I waited in trepidation.

On my next trip to London, the first thing I did was to see St. Jacques!

It was a good production, not a good film, in particular not good for Singapore's image. But Raffles' was clean. I was relieved.

A few years later, I had an unexpected visit. Pathi the thamby told me that a couple insisted on seeing me. There he was - Ben Gazzara and his latest girlfriend. He hugged me as if I were his brother. He told me that he could not resist the temptation of visiting Raffles again, even for a few hours. So on his way back to Europe after a holiday in Bali, he made a special stopover in Singapore. He also said that he was worried of being detained by the police for his role in St. Jacques. However this was a minor risk in his life.

The policewoman at the airport was friendly, smiling. She even said "Enjoy your holiday in Singapore". Most probably she had never seen any of his movies. We spent five hours at the Palm Court talking. Then I drove them to the airport.

Ben Gazzara is still my favourite actor and best friend.

Franco Indovina was another famous film producer who came to Raffles.

He came incognito and called me from the airport. He wanted me to assure him absolute privacy and no publicity at all. His partner was none other than the ex-Empress of Iran, Soraya - a beautiful but most sad and unlucky lady. Indovina also asked my wife to be the chaperon for Soraya during her stay. My wife was indeed very honoured.

I think for every lady, an Empress is the epitome of aspiration, envy and admiration.

Soraya enjoyed my wife's company and when she learned that her Chinese name was Jade she bought her a jade pendant in appreciation.

Before leaving, Indovina and Soraya invited us to their home in Rome.

Unfortunately Indovina died a few months later in a plane crash near Palermo.

Another sad story for the most beautiful Empress.

Now, how to describe Bernardo Bertolucci? He too came to Raffles. After *The Last Tango in Paris*, I didn't know whether it was to escape the court case or to find inspiration for a new film.

He was Italian and when Italians meet overseas they become good friends.

Bertolucci came with an English girlfriend and I gave him our best suite, where Ava Gardner, Claudia Cardinale and Robert Kennedy had slept, and the secret love between Hayley Mills and Roy Boulting had blossomed.

The next morning, the guest who stayed exactly below them made a strong complaint to the reception that someone above his room must have danced the whole night on the floor as well as on the bed. I smiled. Most probably the producer of the Last Tango in Paris was practising for a new film, *The Last Ronggeng* in Singapore.

During his stay in Singapore, Bertolucci wanted to visit the real Chinatown. He asked my wife to take them along to explain the colourful traditions of Sago Lane, the Chinese medicine shops and the opium dens. Maybe it was here that the "Last Emperor" was conceived.

They went to a Chinese sinseh who happened to be my wife's friend. There, after a long explanation on the aphrodisiac effects of certain Chinese medicines, Bertolucci bought two horned toads which were supposed to be good for sex. "For a newly married friend," he said, with a grin.

A Most Stubborn Ghost

Ghosts were among my favourite guests. They never complained. The only problem was that they made my guests complain on their behalf.

Here is a letter from a Mr. Trickey about ghosts at Raffles.

To The Manager of Raffles Hotel,

> *Dear Sir,*
> *Last week, the BBC broadcast a story about a ghost who lives in your hotel.*
> *For some time. I have had an especial interest in ghosts and have taken action to help them to be somewhere else. That action isn't, in any way, connected with the pagan ritual of exorcism which professes to banish to outer darkness or to 'the place appointed for evil spirits or forces ...*
> *On Tuesday. 15th January at about 4 a.m. your time and the presence of two other people, I carried out a rescue action for your ghost: something I hadn't previously attempted over such a long distance. I hope that you will understand the motives in so doing. If you could agree that, in the interest of the 'personality', it was right to do so, I would appreciate your letting me know whether it has ceased to be present. Only by cessation or continuance of its presence can one know whether the action has or has not been successful.*
> *Yours Sincerely*
> *EJ Trickey Sommerset*
> *England*
> *23rd January 1985*

And here is how I replied:

> *Dear Mr. Trickey.*
> *I wish to thank you for your rescue action and congratulate you for your successful attempt over such a long distance. Somerset Maughamn. Rudyard Kipling, and Joseph Conrad would have agreed that it was their best interest to do so.*
> *Whether the action has been successful or no, would depend on Dr. & Mrs. Peterson who have just checked into the Somerset Maugham Suite.*
> *Yours truly*
> *Roberto Pregarz*

Kermit Meets A Girlfriend

During the Singapore Festival of Arts, we had a bevy of film producers, film stars, rising stars ... They all had a common wish - to come to Raffles.

I organized colonial parties, tea parties, candlelight parties and once even a breakfast party.

At first they were not so keen to get up so early after a night at the theatre and then Bugis Street, but that was their last chance before leaving, so they came to Raffles. Among the 20 or more brave and famous stars was Jim Henson. The reporters, photographers and TV crew were invited too, to interview these stars, but they chose only one. The star of the stars - Kermit the Frog. I was told that Mr. Jim Henson never leaves Kermit at home alone. So Kermit the Frog was being interviewed in the centre of the Palm Court. He was choosy. He wanted a nice spot to take home a photo as a souvenir.

My daughter Lisa (aged four) came to see what her daddy was doing.

She saw me, then she saw Kermit. She was very excited. "Papa, look, Kermit the Frog. I want to see, I want to see."

It wasn't so easy to approach Kermit with so many reporters around. I had an idea. I rushed to Lisa's room, I took her Puppet "Tiga", a tiger cub and rushed back to give it to Lisa. From behind the shoulders, Lisa, No! Tiga waved to Kermit.

Kermit blinked an eye, left the reporters spellbound, and went to meet Tiga

... Another love blossomed at Raffles.

Jim Henson,
Kermit the Frog,
Elisabetta and
Tiga the tiger

Raffles Treasures

When I joined Raffles, it took me several days to find my way around. Although the buildings of Raffles are only three storeys high, there are almost three kilometers of corridors.

On the backyard of the hotel I found several locked rooms, but I could not find any keys. Nobody had opened these rooms for several years. Someone told me that inside there were ghosts and that the Japanese had used the rooms for interrogation.

One day I could not resist my curiosity so, with the help of Ah Tuck, the carpenter, I opened the doors of these rooms.

In one I found trunks belonging to our old guests which were half eaten by cockroaches and white ants. In another I found old Raffles furniture. Some were very plain, I believe they must have been made around 1935. But a few must have been of an earlier period because they had some nice carving like those I saw in photographs of the 1920's. These pieces had several coats of paint, white, blue, green. Luckily these layers of paint had saved them from the jaws of the termites.

But the most exciting discovery was in another room. Here I found thousands of pieces of silverware, most badly corroded and black stained. There were cutlery, bowls, dishes, wine stands, cruets and other very unusual pieces which I have never seen around.

It was very interesting that some had the logo of the Sarkies Brothers on and also those of the Strand Hotel in Rangoon and of the E & 0 in Penang which also belonged to the Sarkies.

After polishing and re-silver-plating them, some of these precious pieces were returned for display in the Elizabethan Grill together with the famous silver wagon.

This precious piece of silverware was unearthed immediately after the Japanese surrendered! This is what happened:

This piece of silverware was the proud display of the Raffles Grill in the pre-war days.

During each banquet it was brought into the Grill by the Bagpipers. After the master of ceremonies' announcements, the guest-of-honour proudly carved the beef which was later served to the diners.

Each occasion was of course immortalized by photos. Who was taking these photos?

Nakajima, the official Raffles photographer, whose shop was in the premises.

When the Japanese invaded Singapore Nakajima returned to Raffles as a Lieutenant Colonel of the Imperial Japanese army. The first thing he did when he came to Raffles was to look for the "silver wagon". He searched for it in vain for three years. Some of Raffles' faithful waiters had buried the wagon and other silverware in the Palm Court only hours before the Japanese invasion. Later these waiters were interned in Changi Prison and fortunately Colonel Nakajima could not locate and question them.

To his extreme disappointment, the Raffles silver wagon is now still proudly displayed in the Raffles Grill.

With the increasing popularity of Raffles, "the interest in items" with the Raffles crest grew too.

Not only the consumption of stirrers, coasters, matches, increased beyond normal business requirement, but also silver teaspoons. Silver salt and pepper sets, silver lemon squeezers etc. started to "disappear". One can see this from

The Elizabethan Grill Staff with the Silver Wagon

two points of view: one as a loss, and the other as tremendous publicity.

But I saw the opportunities! I ordered extra pieces from the manufacturer. I opened a little souvenir shop and sold them.

I got the benefits of profit, publicity and free replacements.

The "Little Shop" souvenir business grew to a quarter million Singapore dollars per month.

Could you imagine the "losses" if I had not have started the "Little Shop"?

When a couple in the Elizabethan Grill asked to see the Manager, I wondered whether it was to make a complaint or to make a compliment. None of these!

When they saw me they placed something on the table wrapped in old Chinese newspapers. They unwrapped it and out came a beautiful silver warmer with the crest of Raffles Hotel of the 1930's.

I didn't dare ask if they had stolen it. They would not have shown it to me if they had.

They told me that they had just come back from the Thieves Market at Rochore Canal. There they saw this beautiful piece of silver in very good condition, so they bought it for S$100, after a bit of bargaining.

I thought that they might want to sell it to me and make a good profit. New it was worth over S$600 and antique much, much more. How much?

They felt that it wasn't right for them to keep it, for it belonged to Raffles.

"Return to me the S$ l00 and it is yours!" they said.

This is how much our guests appreciate Raffles!

Announcing the arrival of London's Lord Mayor

The Tiffin Room

... over 1200 Singapore Sling per day

The Elizabethan Grill

Books about Raffles Hotel

There is only one Raffles
by Ilsa Sharp
Raffles The Story of Singapore
by Raymond Flower
Year of the Tiger, Centenary of Raffles
by Raymond Flower
Raffles Treasury
by Andreas Augustin
221 Raffles
by Russel Foreman
Memories of Raffles
by Roberto Pregarz
Tiger's Tale
by Kelly Chopard
Raffles, The Untold Story
by George
The Original Singapore Sling
by Goh Eck Kheng
Raffles, the Songbirds of Singapore
by Marilyn and Wayne Levy
Raffles Hotel
by Gretchen Liu

... will I be a writer?

Raymond Flower, Russell Foreman and William Golding

Ilsa Sharp

Noel Barber

Mr. and Mrs. James Michener Welcome to your second home, Raffles!

Gavin Young and Roberto exchanging their books

Left:
Mrs. Mary Wilson & Mrs.Lee Kuan Yew

Right:
President of Ireland

Left:
Mr Wu Xue Qian
Foreign Minister of People Republic of China

Right:
Mr Cyrus Vance
USA Secretary of State

Left:
H. E. Valerie Giscard D'Estaing
President of France

Right:
Lord Mountbatten
of Burma

Left:
Princess Sonia
of Norway

Right:
H.E. Francesco Cossiga
President of Italy

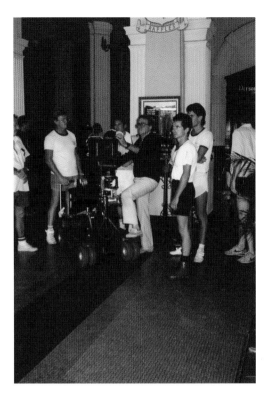

Filming **Passion Flower**
with Bruce Boxleitner
and Barbara Ashley

Filming **Tanamera**

57

Peter Graves

George Hamilton

Jean Paul Belmondo

Japanese models

Bjon Borg

Miss Raffles

With her two Chaperons

Miss Raffles

Usually one would associate Raffles with elderly conservative patrons: characters coming straight out of a Somerset Maugham short story, or from a Noel Coward play, but not necessarily as the "mad dogs and Englishman" type.

One imagines them sitting on the breezy verandah and calling:

Boy! Bring me a stengah! And a gin pahit for me!

Did you hear about Mrs. Proudlock and her lover?

… And waiting for the thambi to bring the mail from home which had just arrived on the P & 0 steamer after calling at Bombay, Rangoon and Penang.

So it was quite a refreshing whirlwind when 35 of the most beautiful women in the world competing for the coveted title of Miss Universe 1988 invaded Raffles.

They paraded in swimsuits in the Palm Court - one could almost see Somerset Maugham peeping out from a window and conjuring another story.

The pageant was televised around the hotel and only Raffles could provide an instant identity for Singapore for the worldwide audience.

When the parade of these ladies started, life at Raffles stopped. There was no staff in the kitchen. no customers in the restaurants. Everybody rushed to get the best view of the Palm Court or a better view of these beauties. I even saw some of my maintenance staff on the roof.

Every camera in the hotel was pointed at these beautiful representatives of the world.

Suddenly, while a group of these young ladies were trying to outdo each other in front of the TV cameras, an unexpected new contestant appeared wearing a flimsy bikini.

"Wow!" everybody exclaimed.

"She is the most beautiful"

And all the cameras and attention turned towards her. I too was attracted by this sudden commotion and I went to see who she was.

Who did I find?

My three year old daughter, Elisabetta, who had been dressed up (or undressed) by my housekeeping staff Miss Lim, Susan, Lin Choo, Patricia and Hairani.

They made her wear a bikini, put some nice make-up and lipstick on her face, put a garland of orchids around her neck and gave her a sash with "Miss Raffles" written on it.

She was really the most beautiful!

Suddenly the cameras began to focus on my-our Miss Raffles!

Even Stamford Raffles and the Sarkies would have agreed.

A Staircase Just For Fun

Our Palm Court has a beautiful pateo. It has been photographed or filmed by almost every visitor. This patio was also selected as a background for the beautiful contestants to the title of Miss Universe 1987.

But one thing I hated about it was - the staircase, which must have been designed by someone who specialized in air raid shelters.

Just behind Raffles Hotel there was a beautiful old theatre - The Jubilee. It was named after the Jubilee of Queen Victoria celebrated in 1895. Passing by, I used to admire the two (20 ft high) beautiful wrought-iron spiral staircases, one on each side of the building, leading to the balcony.

After the theatre closed down, the building started to deteriorate rapidly, and a banyan tree started to clasp and embrace it tightly.

Each time I passed by the theatre, I dreamt that one day I could reopen it with my favourite Noel Coward shows.

Months, and then years passed. The building deteriorated further. One day I noticed that the steps of the beautiful winding staircases started to disappear. My appeal to the owners failed to save the staircases. So, with the complicity of the demolition contractor the last few remaining steps disappeared.

A few days later the last remnants of the staircases made a magical appearance in the Palm Court.

Out of the remnants of the two staircases I managed to build one but unfortunately it was just too short to reach the first floor. Instead it was placed somewhere at the side of the lawn leading to nowhere.

Just as the Fiddler on the Roof would have "one staircase going up, one staircase going down, and one more, going nowhere, just for fun",

Raffles had now realized the Fiddler's dream.

The Palm Court

The beautiful wrought-iron spiral staircase always a haunt for souvenir-snap shots

Just An Ordinary Couple Who One Day ...

During my 22 years at Raffles, I encountered all sorts of guests, pleasant, nasty, demanding, insolent, appreciative, rich, bankrupts, crooks, preachers, dealers in firearms.

But if I have to point out which one stood most prominently in my mind, it would be a nice elderly couple who spent about 10 years at Raffles after their retirement.

They were extremely kind to me and to the staff. They were most generous, not demanding at all. If they wanted a new set of curtains, they would buy it. They paid their bills promptly. They never complained. Even when the lift broke down and it took two weeks to get it repaired, they said: "A bit of exercise is good for us." They were also very caring.

One day, I told them that we were going on a holiday to Europe to visit my parents. At that time we did not have any children but we had two Siamese cats. The first thing they said was, "Roberto, can you do us a favour. Can we look after your cats while you are away? We love cats. Unfortunately when we gave up our company's house and decided to live in a hotel, we gave away our cat too. We loved him." My wife and I were more than happy. They did us a great favour! During our holiday in Europe we received a postcard from them every week.

Dear Roberto and Helena.
Your cats are so sweet. They enjoy sitting on our silk chairs and sometimes they sleep with us. The hotel is okay. Have a nice holiday!
Eric and Biddy

Three lines about the cats, three words about the hotel.

When we returned from our holiday we were happy, but the Berrills were sad because they had to part with the cats, but we made them happy again when we let them spend at least an hour a day with our cats.

Two years later we went on a holiday again. The same thing happened. The Berrills looked after the cats and continued to send us postcards until one day, they sent us a letter.

I was in my hometown in Trieste and driving a rented car when I saw the postman waving at me. I stopped and he gave me a letter. My wife opened it and read it while I was driving along.

Dear Helena and Roberto,
Thought you would like to know how things are going along here. All is well except for the fire on the first floor last weekend. Only three rooms were completely destroyed & the painters & the workmen think they can get the other rooms repaired & operational again in about six week.
A coconut in the Palm Court fell on an American having dinner the other night & he's in hospital, but the hotel's insurance has this well in hand. This was the same night when there was trouble in the bar. Two sailors knocked out Tan Chin Tuan and broke his jaw. Irene & Mrs. Vayloo have gone for a short trip to Japan — we miss them, it seems a little short staffed now that William Wee has left — I say 'left', but he had to as he is now in prison for driving his new red car around the National Stadium at over 100 mph and ruining the football field — but there is absolutely nothing at all for you to worry about & we hope you are having a wonderful time — of course the pussies are fine.
With all our best wishes
Eric and Biddy

At the end of the letter, my wife laughed and I too, then I started to think - the Berrills writing this? Well, they are nice, friendly, but did they ever joke with us? No! Never!

Coconuts falling on guests' heads!

Didn't we cut the fruit from the trees recently? No!

Mr. Wee in prison for racing? Cannot be! But he did buy a racing car! To drive slowly? No!

Fire in the room? Well we had a few small fires but I handled them. Yes, I did promptly, but this time I wasn't there. I arrived home. I tried to park the car, I banged into the gate, I broke a light. was trembling, pale as a ghost.

Helena said, "Don't worry. We will call Singapore and you'll see that it's joke."

I picked up the phone, ready to dial ... But what was Raffles' number? I forgot! I looked into my diary, I found my Chairman's number. First I called him; "He is not at home" replied his amah. I called my secretary next on my direct line. No answer. 1.00 p.m. in Italy, 7.00 p.m. in Singapore. Of course she was not in. Then I tried Raffles! Line engaged. Dammed old switchboard!

I told my wife, "Sorry I can't take the risk. Let me call the airline first and book a seat for tomorrow to Singapore". I called the airline - No answer - Lunch time.

I called Raffles again, this time I got through. The first thing I asked was, "Is everything all right?" "Yes, Mr. Pregarz, I think so."

"Think so? Give me the Assistant Manager."

"Sorry he is sick."

"Give me the Supervisor."

"Sorry, he is out for a meeting."

Sigh! Dear me, "Give me Mr. Berrill."

"Hello! Mrs. Berrill here, Who is it? Roberto! Oh, did you have a good holiday? Are you back already? We didn't expect you so soon." -

"No I am in Italy".

"Don't worry, the cats are fine."

Don't worry? "I am not asking about the cats! What about the fire? The coconut? Mr. Wee?"

"What? Oh dear me, Eric, what did we do? We had too many drinks that night, I told you not to do such a thing. Sorry Roberto, we are awfully sorry. We didn't know you would take it so seriously. We got drunk that night when we wrote you that letter!"

"Never mind," I said, "thank you for the cats!"

I too got drunk after that phone call.

Exposed At Raffles In Six Acts

What Iris Forbes, Noel Coward, Miss Penaligon, Liz Taylor, three Swedish blondes and Botticelli's Venus had in common was that all of them exposed a bit more flesh than one would expect at Raffles.

Act 1: "POLICE BAN TO STAND" was reported in the Straits Times in 1938.

"The Singapore police ban on the Whip Dance of an Australian Cabaret artist, Billy Heaton at Raffles Hotel, in which his partner, 19-year-old Iris Forbes, is "flogged" with a long stock-whip, has not been lifted. The ban was imposed on the act by the police after its performance at Raffles Hotel on Friday night, following complaints". The complaint was, that it was not nice for the Chinese hotel servants to witness a white woman being mistreated! Iris Forbes herself wrote to me in 1987, "Of course, I was not hurt by the whip!"

Act 2: Noel Coward must have been the first streaker in the world, when one night in an eccentric mood he ran along the Palm Court chasing his ... "cat" over the garden wall"

Act 3: Raffles is a paradise for photographers and Miss Penaligon must have been Eve for Duffy, the world famous stars' photographer. He changed the setting slightly. Paradise became the Palm Court. And the apple became the Singapore Sling. My not so young conservative housekeeper who was passing by, saw this, and quickly ran to my office mumbling that someone was posing almost naked in the Palm Court in full view of several trishaw riders who were fighting behind the fence to enjoy the best show.

Act 4: Liz Taylor had shown a flash of flesh and blamed Doris Geddes and the zip.

Act 5: Our reception counter never had air-conditioning - only high, old, ceiling fans. However, tradition required our receptionists to wear jackets. In order to improve the ventilation, I created an open concept for the reception. I removed all the partitions and opened the windows overlooking the Palm Court. and since then, no more receptionist had resigned. In a corner of the Palm Court was the swimming pool, and the receptionists had a panoramic view.

One hot afternoon, my front office manager who, prior to joining Raffles, had pursued an ecclesiastic career, came quite excited to my office and asked me to follow him to the swimming pool. He said that three blonde young ladies were enjoying the tropical sun wearing flimsy mono-kinis and they were disturbing the concentration of his receptionists.

Susie Penaligon

MISS IRIS FORBES

Police Ban To Stand

THE Singapore police ban on the whip dance of an Australian cabaret artist, Billy Heaton, at Raffles Hotel, in which his partner, 19-year-old Iris Forbes, is "flogged" with a long stock-whip, has not been lifted.

The ban was imposed on the act by the police after its performance at Raffles Hotel on Friday night, following complaints.

The artist forgot to colour the important parts
Andrea and Bryan finished the job

Act 6: We Italians love art.

Over the years we had collected three beautiful statues for our Palm Court - two marble cupids and one copy of Venus by Botticelli from his painting, "The Birth of Venus". Around this last statue we built a pond where we put some colourful tropical fishes.

My son Andrea (5 years old) and his best friend Bryan (4 years old) were cute as well as mischievous. More than once I had caught them playing in the pond with their battery boats, chasing the fishes.

One evening, my wife, our two children and I were having dinner at the Palm Court when one of the waitresses, who was serving Singapore Slings to a group of tourists seated near the statue of Venue, noticed that her private parts (of Venus, not hers) had been painted black and rushed to report to us.

I went to see. It was true. I tried to wash it but the colour didn't come out. It was embarrassing when I realised the group of tourists were watching in amusement, me — the Manager performing my act. My wife commented that it was disgraceful to do such a thing. How could one vandalise "Venus" at Raffles?

"But mama," my son said, "the person who made the statue forgot to colour the teats and the hair down below, so my friend, Bryan and I finished the job." True Italian blood!

Next morning, they were sent to the pond with the fire hose and brushes to undo what they had done as nobody wanted to be seen performing the ticklish job!

Some Of The Most Notable Patrons Of The Elizabethan Grill

This well renowned restaurant was established only in 1953, sixty six years after Raffles was officially opened. Within a few years. it had gained a reputation not only for good food but also for a series of outstanding events. The restaurant was named in honour of Her Majesty, Queen Elizabeth II of England who was crowned in 1953. At the entrance, proudly displayed, was her portrait painted by Gerald Henderson. One could almost hear mighty echoes of "God Save the Queen" as one looked at her.

Exactly ten years later, suddenly the Elizabethan Grill, including the portrait, disappeared. The next day like magic, a new restaurant opened "The Epicurean Grill". Coincidentally, the menu, the dishes, were the same but the customers had vanished.

A year later, magic again. The Epicurean Grill disappeared and the Elizabethan Grill reopened. The same menu, and the same customers had returned! But the portrait had been changed. This time Gerald Henderson had painted another Elizabeth, a Tudor - the daughter of Henry VIII and Anne Boleyn. She was vain, difficult and headstrong (all qualities which my daughter Elisabetta had inherited), but she nevertheless had a very shrewd instinct about the country's strength and weakness, and she identified herself with her realm as no previous ruler had done.

Years later, the Lion of Judah with his tiny Chihuahua dog made an interim entrance to this restaurant.

Raffles had its first imperial banquet in honour of his Imperial Majesty Haille Selassie.

The Emperor's chihuahua was the only privileged puppy, not only to enter the Elizabethan Grill but to have its meal next to the fire place. Accidentally one of the old waiters, whilst serving the Emperor kicked the puppy. It yelled and the Emperor's bodyguards drew their guns. A few months later the Emperor was dethroned.

The next prominent personality to have banqueted at the Elizabethan Grill, was H.E. Pierre Trudeau, Prime Minister of Canada. He laughed when he was told the story about Selassie. Incidentally a few months later he too lost his job.

See who was next?

When Singapore hosted the Commonwealth Prime Ministers Conference in 1971, a few Heads of State were hosted together in the Elizabethan Grill. After the desserts there was a trunk call for H.E. Milton Obote, Prime Minister of Uganda. He was politely informed that there would be another Prime Minister in his country. Three was supposed to be enough but ...

Next to try the hospitality of the Elizabethan Grill was President Zia of Bangladesh. A few months later, he was shot.

Enough is enough!

Yet we saw a report from the Business Times, Thursday, February 25, 1988 Raffles to be closed and turned into a "suites only" hotel for VIP Guests and "Heads of State"!

The legend of the Elizabethan Grill must go on for a sequel, for a renaissance ...

When the hotel re-opened in 1991 the new owners decided not to take any chances and they renamed it the Raffles Grill.

Emperor Haille Selassie being hosted to a state dinner at the Elizabethan Grill
by Chief Justice and Mrs. Wee Chong Jin and Dr. Goh Keng Swee

"Almost all restaurants forbid the presence of pets.
Not, unfortunately, in some parts of the Far East, where a visiting couple, accompanied by
a plump poodle were served with a lavish meal, and explained to the waiter in universal
sign language, they wanted him to feed the animal, as well.
He nodded and beamed before taking the dog off in the direction of the kitchens.
Thirty minutes later, he returned, bearing on a large silver platter
the delicately roasted pet on a bed of crispy noodles."

An Unusual Request

"Mr. Pregarz!" The Front Office Manager rang me late in the evening "Sorry to disturb you at this hour, but there is a lady in her room who just checked in. She refuses to go to bed until she talks to you."

"Okay", I said, half asleep. "Put me through to her."

"Yes, Mrs. Morrison, (I always made it a point to find out the names of my guests). Can I help you?"

"Are you the manager?" she asked.

"Yes!" I said.

"Well, it is time that you learn how to operate this hotel and make sure that your guests have all the comfortable amenities".

"Yes, may I know what is wrong?" I said, "Is the air-conditioning not working?"

"No, I am not talking about that! When I was here last time in 1937 some 40 years ago my room had a mosquito-net, and I cannot sleep without one."

"Well, Mrs. Morrison, mosquitoes are not allowed in our country, especially in this hotel. If the authorities find some we shall be heavily fined."

"Allowed or not, I want my mosquito-net back!" said Mrs. Morrison. "Please give me a bit of time and I'll fix one for you in an hour." I replied.

I got out of bed. I went to the reception to find if any lady member of the staff was still working. I found one and I asked her if she could sew. She said, "yes". So we went to the linen room and took some old net curtains and she sewed a mosquito-net. I took a hook and went to hang the mosquito net above Mrs. Morrison's bed and we tied some ribbons to make it look pretty.

"I take back my words!" said Mrs. Loretta Morrison. "This is what I call good service, but make sure that the next time I come back, the mosquito-net is there!"

Mrs. Morrison was in her 70s. In any case I wouldn't dream of removing it.

Year Of The Dragon

February 1988 - Finally the most auspicious Chinese New Year, the Year of the Dragon, had arrived - the best of the 12 years of the Chinese zodiac.

It was not only because it brings good luck and comes only once in 12 years, but this particular one with a lucky combination of four 8s comes only once in many centuries (8/8/88).

I missed to be a dragon by just a few days, so I am a rabbit. My parents fault. They had no Chinese education. My consolation was that my birthday fell twice during the Year of the Dragon.

Raffles is international, is multi-religious, is multi-cultural and is multi-national. At Raffles I used every opportunity to generate business, so we celebrated Christmas - New Year - Chinese New Year - Hari Raya - Deepavali - Stamford Raffles' Landing anniversary - Opening of Raffles Hotel anniversary, Queen Jubilee, you name it! I did it!

At Raffles, for the year of the Dragon which started on 15th February 1988, we had two giant dragons to welcome this auspicious year. One made of styrofoam, was placed right at the entrance of the hotel to welcome our guests. The other one was a special dragon dance with a 50 metre long silk dragon.

After the performance in the lobby the dragon went around the hotel to chase all the evil spirits and ended up at the Writers Bar, not for a cocktail prepared by Mr. How Wee How, the head barman, but to wish one of our most notable writers "Kong Xi Fa Cai" or Happy New Year.

Noel Barber with wife Titina and the director of Tanamera

This writer was none other than Noel Barber who came to Raffles with his wife, Titina, to meet an Australian producer ... who was planning a television series for one of Noel Barber's most popular novels - Tanamera. There was no better place to meet than at Raffles, no more auspicious day to plan this movie than the 15th of February 1988- The first day of the Year of the Golden Dragon.

It was a great pity that Noel Barber could not come to Singapore in June the same year to supervise the filming. He, unfortunately had died. But his legacy at Raffles remains with Tanamera.

I Want To See The Manager

I am an early riser. I got this habit from working on the ship. 5.30 am. "Wake up!" First with a whistle, then a glass of water not to be drunk but to be poured on your face if you were still found in bed after five minutes.

But at Raffles, I truly enjoyed getting up early in the morning with the friendly call of the two golden orioles perched on the orange-berried Livinstona palm tree just outside our window.

Then I went to take my breakfast at the Palm Court and to listen to Mr. Ho's singing birds. Some of my assistants used to come early too, either attracted by the singing birds or to avoid paying for the CBD pass. I think for both.

There was no better way to start the day. After breakfast I went straight to my deserted peaceful office to do my paperwork and to make my plans for the day. I usually was left in peace from 7.30 to 9 a.m. No secretary, no telephone calls, just quietness.

After 9 a.m. the Manager of Raffles is at the mercy of his guests and telephone calls.

Amazing how many guests wanted to meet the Manager of Raffles. Not Roberto Pregarz, but the Manager of Raffles whoever he may be.

The first person to make me realize how important was the Manager of Raffles, was my Chairman.

One day I suggested to him that because of the increased popularity of Raffles and the interest shown by journalists and VIPs, it might be feasible to engage a public relations officer who was more qualified for this job than me. I am Italian, my English pronunciation hadn't made progress even though I married an English— literature graduate teacher.

"Roberto", my Chairman said, "the guests or the journalists don't want to meet a public relations officer, as cute and pretty as she may be, or as good English-speaking as she may be. They want to meet and to talk to the Manager of Raffles."

"Yes Sir! I understand!"

One day, just before my secretary arrived, one of our regular guests came to my office.

My door was always kept open.

"Mr. Pregarz," he said, "I am taking up an appointment in Saudi Arabia and my wife has just got a baby. I think I would prefer my wife to stay here while I settle down there. What do you think?"

What do I think? was a hard question for a hotel manager to answer. "Well," I said "If you prefer to go alone I assure you that she and the baby would be safe here and well looked after until you decide to call for them."

One week later, I received a cable from Saudi Arabia.

"Kindly inform Mrs. Smith that her husband has died of a heart attack." Did he have a premonition?

To tell the lady this sad news wasn't quite an easy job but it had to be done. I did it with the help of my wife and my housekeeper.

Later in the day chief cashier Mr. Tan who had been working for Raffles since 1936 and who worked at Raffles even during the Japanese Occupation rushed to me and excitedly told me that there was a group of elderly Japanese touring the hotel.

"What's so special?" I said, "We have dozens of groups each day."

"Oh no", he said, "among them I recognize an officer who stayed at Raffles in 1944."

I rushed there to interview him to enhance my historical collection. What a great opportunity, I thought. Unfortunately, he disappeared among the crowd.

While I was still there at the reception I saw a lady complaining to the front office manager that someone had stolen all her jewellery which she had worn the night before at a party.

I went to her room with the housekeeper, the front office manager and a security officer to make a search. We could not find the jewellery. A maid confirmed that she saw the lady wearing the jewellerv when she left for the party and this made it worse. We searched every corner and at the end I had to call the police to look for fingerprints.

The lady was furious and wanted to sue us for her missing diamonds and pearls. What could I do? So I returned to my office to write a report for the insurance claim.

Then suddenly, there was our faithful Mary who had been in charge of the guests laundry for over 30 years. In one hand she had an evening gown, and in the other the jewellery. She got so excited when she saw so much jewellery that she rushed to me.

The guest after enjoying a few million-dollar cocktails had placed her evening dress on top of the laundry basket and hidden the jewellery inside a sleeve, just in case.

In the morning when this lady went down to the Palm Court for breakfast, the chambermaid made her room and took the laundry basket and the dress to the laundry.

Another problem of the day solved!

The Palm Court

Fond Memories Of Raffles

The traditionalists— he's delving into the niceties of tea dance and tiffin (and maybe an odd gin sling) and she's busy preserving *baba nonya* cooking to keep old ideas alive

Roberto Pregarz, the general manager of the famous ninety-year-old Raffles Hotel.

In 1886 three Armenian brothers called Sarkies took over a "tiffin house" on the Singapore waterfront and opened the Raffles Hotel. They also built the Strand in Rangoon and the E & O in Penang—but those two grand old ladies never achieved the international fame and literary inspiration of Raffles.

"Raffles stands for all the fables of the exotic East," wrote Somerset Maugham stayed there in 1919 and forty years. In tr would

Mrs. Lee Chin Koon, cookery expert, and mother of Singapore's Prime Minister.

Matchmakers have always played an important role in Asia—and none more so than among the strictly traditional *Baba Nonyas* (Straits-born Chinese who adopted Malay customs over the past four hundred years).

The matchmaker would walk through the *kampong* (village) at about ten in the morning and listen intently to the rhythms of pounding with pestle and mortar. From this she could tell an experienced cook from a tyro—and cooking skills were the main criterion in a girl's marriage chances.

Baba Nonyas are a unique breed whose history is also the history of Chinese migration to Singapore, Malacca and Penang. *Babas* (the men) came as labourers and craftsmen in those early days, and many married Malay women, adopting their customs, cooking and dress and dropping their native dialects in favour of Malay. *Nonyas* (the women) are renowned for their intricate, spicy cooking and old-fashioned manners which are quite contrary to Chinese good manners.

Mrs Lee Chin Koon is the region's foremost expert on all aspects of *Baba Nonya* tradition: she is also mother of Prime Minister Lee Kwan Yew—but she prefers talking about discussing her privacy-cons

Cooking is a way of

The Managers of Raffles are not only **traditionalists** but also sentimentalists.

I believe I share many common qualities (hopefully the good ones) with Franz Schutzman.

In my opinion and also those of the journalists who had interviewed him, Franz was "The Hotelier"

He was a spy during the war, a controversial journalist, an unprofessional gambler, a great lover and he managed also to become the Manager of Raffles, of the Cavalieri Hilton in Rome, of the United Nation Hyatt in New York, and of the Manila Hotel in the Philippines.

When he invited me to the Manila Hotel, he made me stay in the MacArthur Suite. So, when he came to Singapore I wanted to return the courtesy, hut he refused!

He returned to Raffles unexpectedly in 1983 for the first time after 23 years. Rajoo, the receptionist who had been with Raffles for over 30 years and who used to work for him came to me all excited to tell me that Franz had come back.

I went to see Franz and around him I saw almost every employee who used to work for him.

"I have always had a soft spot for this place" he said. "The minute I walked in I felt as if I was coming home again, and it is very touching to find some of the employees who once worked with me still around".

Unfortunately I had a previous engagement so I could not share memories with Franz that evening. Before dashing out I told him; "Franz, tonight Raffles has no Manager. Would you mind taking over?"

I saw Franz walking through the hallowed portals of Raffles, followed by "his staff' every inch the General Manager and when he turned his face towards me, I saw tears in his eyes filled with fond memories of Raffles.

Franz Schutzman (centre) with Roberto and Tan Geok Swee who joined Raffles in 1936

Raffles .... An Institution

When the Raffles Institution, the school which was founded by Sir Stamford Raffles in 1823, was pulled down, the headlines in major newspapers around the world read: "Raffles Hotel has been pulled down!"

I had a hard time convincing the journalists and friends of Raffles, that was not the Hotel which was pulled down, but the school, the Raffles Institution.

All this Because of Senator
Staniforth Smith statement!
in the Melbourne Argus.

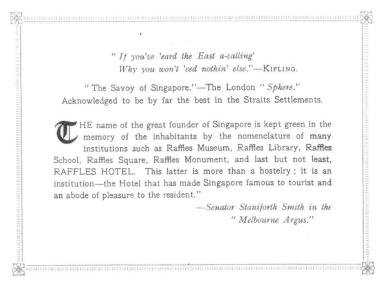

" If you've 'eard the East a-calling'
 Why you won't 'eed nothin' else."—KIPLING.

"The Savoy of Singapore."—The London "Sphere."
Acknowledged to be by far the best in the Straits Settlements.

THE name of the great founder of Singapore is kept green in the memory of the inhabitants by the nomenclature of many institutions such as Raffles Museum, Raffles Library, Raffles School, Raffles Square, Raffles Monument, and last but not least, RAFFLES HOTEL. This latter is more than a hostelry ; it is an institution—the Hotel that has made Singapore famous to tourist and an abode of pleasure to the resident."

—Senator Staniforth Smith in the
"Melbourne Argus."

And this was followed up later ...

The first international institution to officially recognize Raffles Hotel as a Singapore's heritage was American Express.

Mr. Stephen Halsey, President of the American Express Foundation and Mr. Barry Arnold, Vice President for the area were the persons behind the dedication of the "Heritage Plaque" to the hotel. This dedication placed Raffles among the most historical institutions in the world, as a recognition for Raffles Hotel's contribution to the promotion of tourism through historical heritage.

Mrs. Halsey inspired me to create the Raffles Table for lonely travellers to meet and to exchange their love stories of Raffles.

The Day A Trishaw Ride Man Became A Knight

Trishaws and rickshaws have been closely associated with Raffles as well as with myself. When Raffles opened its doors, the first guests were brought in on our rubber-tyred jinrickshaws. When somebody misspelled it as "gin rickshaw" it was thought that this was the kind of energy required to pull the heavy "ang mo" (white man).

On the day Prime Minister Lee Kuan Yew was born, rickshaws stole the limelight in the front page of the Straits Times. The rickshaw pullers were not celebrating Mr. Lee's birth, but were fighting over the control of the valuable parking rights in front of Raffles Hotel.

After the invasion of Malaya by the Japanese troops on bicycles, these enterprising warriors developed the "trishaw" by attaching a bicycle to the rickshaw. The trishaw is synonymous with Singapore and is a very popular and economical way of transportation. When the first tourists spotted it they were instantly captivated and so some enterprising trishaw riders started to take tourists around.

The most popular starting point of course for these tours became Raffles. The first tours went to Chinatown and Sago Lane - famous for its funeral parlours with all the related paraphernalia. Some of these tourists gave generous tips to the trishaw riders; those who did not were sent off with colourful descriptions of their close relatives in Chinese dialects.

Some of the tourists were not very knowledgeable of the values of various currencies, American, Canadian, Australian, Singapore, Hong Kong dollars. But the uneducated trishaw riders were! So when the tourists asked "How much for that trishaw ride?" the trishaw man said "$10". When the tourist gave SING$10 the trishaw man complained, but when the tourist gave US$10 the trishaw rider thanked him profusely and quickly rode away. These tricks had annoyed the authorities. It also upset Singaporean users of trishaws who found it more difficult to get one and who also found the fare getting much more expensive. The authorities were also upset by these kings of the roads who, at the traffic junctions became colour blind. They could see only green. They also used to ride without lights at night, but this was not a problem since you could hear them 1/2 mile away because of their blaring "ghetto blaster" sets. Riding a trishaw with this music was similar to riding on a gondola in Venice, only less romantic and more scary.

When I heard that these trishaw riders were about to lose their licence, I was worried that I might lose the Singapore Sling business from these trishaw tours.

So I called some of these trishaw riders for a meeting and told them that it would be better for them to follow these simple rules in order to get some sympathy from the police:

I. Charge the tourists in Singapore dollars.

2. Put on a fresh T-shirt every day

3. Study the highway code.

4, Take a small insurance, just in case.

They survived, and I got promoted by the local press to "Trishaw Ride Man Became A Knight". Then, I don't know why, I was demoted to trishaw puller: The first guests I took around the hotel on a rickshaw was none other than Mr. Raffles, not Stamford, but one of his relatives.

My last job as a rickshaw puller was when I took on the rickshaw a couple called Mr. & Mrs. Malone on their wedding night, for they had particularly come to Raffles for a 1920's style reception.

LOCAL NEWS

TRISHAW RIDE MAN MADE A KNIGHT

By Nancy Koh

Roberto Pregarz is the man behind those processions of wide-eyed tourists snaking their way into Chinatown nightly on trishaws.

For this and his other contributions to the hotel industry, he was conferred the title of Cavaliere (the equivalent of English knighthood) by the Italian Government on Italy's National Day.

The decoration was accorded to him and two other Italians—Mr. Mario Guglielmi, a banker, and Mr. Umberto Papa, a timber merchant — for their contributions in promoting two-way trade between Singapore and Italy.

Mr. Roberto, general manager of the historical colonial-style Raffles Hotel, said yesterday: "It is naturally a great honour to me.

"What made it all the more memorable was that when I received the decoration through the Italian Ambassador here last month, my wife Helena and I were both celebrating our fifth wedding anniversary."

Mr. Roberto said he first thought up the idea of organising trishaw processions when one group of tourists pestered him to rent some trishaws for them.

He said: "On that first night-tour to Chinatown, I went along and personally conducted the tour with my knowledge of the place.

"After the trip, the tourists were raving away about the authentic sights that it suddenly dawned on me that there were tremendous possibilities to be tapped here.

"These night-tours are now a regular affair and the record stands at 110 trishaws on one particular procession."

Mr. Roberto arrived in Singapore as the Maitre 'D of the Lloyd Triestino passenger liner and he was offered the post of assistant manager of Raffles by the incumbent general manager.

"I was immediately attracted to the quaint, old-world atmosphere of the hotel but I reserved by decision.

"Six months passed by. Then in February 1967, a few days before my return to Trieste and on my birthday, the Mediterranean was suddenly very rough and I was terribly seasick.

"When I arrived home, I found the contract in the mail along with a ticket to Singapore. I made my decision then and till now, have no regrets," he said.

And to prove it, Mr. Roberto, 35, pulled out his contract which he recently renewed for another three years.

He said: "Although I shall always remain an Italian, I love it here. And having a local-born Chinese wife has enhanced my appreciation of the people, place and culture.

"Apart from durian (still haven't got round to it!), I have got so used to local dishes that I wouldn't travel to Europe without a bottle of sambals and chilli tucked in my suitcase."

As one of the hoteliers who helped launch the Singapore Hotel and Catering School, Mr. Roberto noted with a tinge of sadness that the industry was now "unhealthy."

He said: "Before we only needed 40 per cent to break even but now we need at least 70 per cent in order to do so. This is purely due to the high rate of operating costs.

"However," he ended on a optimistic note, "I think the situation will pick up again in the second half of next year."

● Picture shows Mr. Roberto taking a trishaw ride.

1986 - The Centenary of Raffles - Yes Or No?

When I joined Raffles in 1967, the history of Raffles Hotel consisted of two typewritten pages handed to me by the Company's secretary. It read:

"Raffles was one of the three hotels owned by the Sarkies Brothers (the others being the E & 0 in Penang and the Strand in Rangoon). Raffles was built in 1886 and opened on the 18th of November."

During the subsequent years, I researched the history of Raffles Hotel to develop its business. In 1976 someone reminded me that during this year Raffles should celebrate the 90th anniversary. Thus on the 18th November 1976 I organized a gala dinner in the Tiffin Room with a stage show dedicated to Noel Coward to commemorate this event.

In 1981, after 3 years of extensive research, British-born and Singapore-based writer and journalist, Ilsa Sharp produced the first history of Raffles Hotel entitled, "There is only one Raffles". This quotation became even more outstanding than Somerset Maugham's "Raffles stands for all the fables of the Exotic East". In her book it is stated that Raffles opened its first 40 rooms on 1st December 1887. So 1986 was not the 100th anniversary. But in 1976 we celebrated the 90th Anniversary, so 1976 + 10 = 1986. Dilemma! What shall we do? Italians can be very resourceful, particularly when the tourist industry in Singapore was facing a drop of 43% in the revenue that year

So...

If the 40 rooms of Raffles were opened on 1st December 1887, the Sarkies must have made their plans in 1886! Therefore, the history of Raffles started in 1886! And 1986 was the centenary of Raffles.

Should it be celebrated on 18th November? Only? No, I started in 1985 in December with a countdown, then came the tiger etc, etc ... and it ended in 1987 just before the new Chinese New Year of the Tiger.

It was the longest 100th birthday anniversary year. It lasted almost 400 days! We look forward now to the bicentennial.

Raffles staff posing for the Centenary

100th birthday bash for Raffles Hotel

Report by STELLA DANKER
Picture by LIM SENG TIONG

Bar captain Ho who'll be mixing a "Million Dollar" cocktail.

OUR grand olde dame of hotels, Raffles Hotel, will celebrate her 100th birthday next month with a week of nostalgia, nightly dining to the menus of the 1920s and a dose of charity to show her greatness of spirit.

The highlight of the celebrations from Nov 18 to 23 will be the showing of the 1946 original film version of Somerset Maugham's The Razor's Edge with Tyrone Power and Anne Baxter.

The Razor's Edge — a story of love, wealth and a man's search for faith in the 1920s — is one of Maugham's better-known works and the British writer was, of course, one of the hotel's better-known guests.

The film will be shown at the 20-seat Regency Room nightly from Nov 18 to 22 and will be open to the public, though hotel guests and diners will get priority.

"What better way to celebrate the hotel's special birthday than to remind people of the writers that made Raffles popular all over the world," said its manager since 1972, Mr Roberto Pregarz.

There will also be a Noel Coward Nostalgia show — a 50-minute rendition of Coward's songs written between the 1920s and the 1950s and excerpts from his play Blithe Spirit — by the Stage Club.

One of the songs in the range is the comic anthem of the empire, Mad Dogs and Englishmen, which Coward is said to have written while staying at the Raffles.

The show will be part of the dinner attraction at the outdoor Palm Court over five nights.

Net proceeds from two dinners, on Nov 19 and 20, will go to the Community Chest. The cost of the charity dinner is $150 per person which includes cocktails, dinner, wine, champagne and any other drink.

Even the cocktails at the Raffles have a history. Apart from the 1915-created Singapore Gin Sling, there is the Million Dollar cocktail which Maugham wrote about in 1920 in another famous story, The Letter.

The story was based on a real-life murder — the bizarre end to a love triangle in 1911. Maugham was inspired to write it by tales and gossip told to him while he was staying at the Raffles and particularly by a chatty Mrs Joyce who was famous for her Million Dollar cocktail.

The potent gin and cointreau blend will be mixed by bar captain Ho Wee How, 48, who is himself something of a hotel "relic" having joined as a room boy when he was 13.

Mr Ho remembers that after joining in 1951, he was room boy to Maugham on his month-long visits each year till the last visit in 1959.

It is this sort of history that the hotel founded by the Sarkies Brothers, three Armenians who also set up the Strand Hotel in Rangoon, thrives on, said Mr Pregarz.

Mr Pregarz wants to resurrect more of its old-world charm. He said that negotiations are under way to buy over the Jubilee Theatre at the back which it would restore to stage Noel Coward plays and show films of Maugham's stories.

THE STAGE CLUB

PRESENTS

NOEL COWARD NOSTALGIA

Devised and Directed by

Christopher Allen

In honour of the 100th Anniversary of the Raffles Hotel

Tyrone Power and Anne Baxter in The Razor's Edge

One More Singapore Sling, Please!

Here are some Sling statements with the kind courtesy of the Long Bar's and the Palm Court's distinguished customers.

- As your wife had warned us - "After two, it brings the devil out of you".
- Not as good as in 1913, but then I was on my honeymoon.
- Just what I expected from reading the novels.
- The one I had at the pool at a neighboring hotel tasted like cough medicine.
- Your Gin Sling drunk in such gorgeous surrounding was my idea of paradise.
- I like it very much! *Worth the trip to Singapore just to sample the Singapore Gin Sling! Same again, please!*

This comment came from two British journalists who did exactly that! They flew the Concorde from London to Singapore, spent a few hours at the Long Bar for a couple of Singapore Slings and flew back to London, by courtesy of the P & 0 which had two vacant seats on the Concorde which flew 98 millionaires to join the QE2 in Singapore.

one for Bruce Boxleitner

- *The sling complemented the atmosphere of both the Long Bar and the Palm Court all of which relieved the atmosphere of Singapore.*
- *Crossed the world to have one and it was worth it,*
- *Well, worth leaving mother — country for.*
- *As in days of yore I dreamt of Singapore. Now here on Silverwing I am drinking the Singapore Sling.*
- *A Singapore Sling is like climbing Avers Rock! We have done it!*
- *Completed our brief visit to Singapore, yet given an appetite for more.*

Gloria Chandy wrote in the Sunday Nation about five men who drank 155 Singapore Slings at Raffles.

What she did not tell you was that the five drinkers were none other than the Celtic Footballers, who after drinking those lethal concoctions, no wonder lost the game against the Red Stars the next day. They really saw red.

and one more for Cliff Richards

The Ngiams of Raffles' Long Bar. A family's tradition since the beginning of last century

Dear Editor,

I refer to the *article* in *January 1981 Beam* on the Singapore Sling. I was scoreperson when the 5 gentlemen attempted a record in the Long Bar in October 1977. The number of slings consumed was 115, not 77, we do have a signal record of this (somewhere!)
I personally escorted two of the participants home by car, I can assure you it was an experience I hope never to repeat! Sadly, one of the only two left standing and coherent was an "Aussie" but the other was a Pommie.

Yours sincerely,
J. Greener (Mrs.)

Five men set record for S'pore Sling

Raffles gave birth to the Sling

from page two

Il Singapore Sling del leggendario Raffles

A true Singapore Sling packs considerable punch and you would be ill-advised to consume more than one of them if planning to do anything that requires sustained concentration afterwards.

Singapore Sling—The untold story

By Robin Lynam

Gin — Peter Heering Liqueur, a few drops of Benedictine, a few drops of Cointreau, pineapple and lime juice, Angostura Bitters, a cherry and a pineapple slice — and some—

Raffles has bar that's 'one of best in world'

By LITO GUTIERREZ

Singapore Sling Is Spoken Here

By COLIN CAMPBELL

Correspon

FAMOUS SINGAPORE SLING WAS INVENTED AT RAFFLES

The Sunday Times, June 22, 1986.

ewpoints ▪ Tiresias

Ready to face the world with five Singapore Slings

There Will Always Be A Raffles

Running Raffles was not as smooth as some people may think. When I was the Assistant Manager, I had someone above me to blame for the problems, but when I became the Manager, I got them all on my own and quite a handful too! Read the following headlines:

Now big hotel price war is on!
New Nation April 9, 1972
Hotel industry faces a big crisis.
Asia Hotel, Tourism 1974
Raffles scarcely moving at all.
New Nation 1973
Progress threatens Singapore 's Raffles Hotel.
Montreal Star March 22, 1975
Move to preserve Raffles as a monument.
New Nation August, 1976
Construction boom burying old seductive Singapore.
Evening News 1976
Fears of another glut of rooms.
Business Times October 17, 1977
No more time for fables.
Time Magazine December 29, 1977
Born 1886, Going. going..,?
New Nation April 19, 1979
100 years test for Raffles.
New Nation July 27, 1979
Raffles Hotel at the crossroads.
Business Times March 15
Raffles a race against time.
Travel News Asia May 14
The last ball may be the wreckers ball.
Asian Wall Street Journal
Raffles Hotel location may be redeveloped.
Travel Trade Gazette
Is Raffles under the gun?
Australian Express

It is a pity that I had to worry about the future of Raffles for so many years.

I wished that Singaporean journalist Tan Bah Bah could have discovered this big mix-up earlier. Read what he wrote;

The mix-up over Raffles Hotel

Some time "long ago the government decided not to pull down Raffles Hotel. That is what National Development Minister had said.

A number of freak events took place which prevented the important information from being passed on to the people who were supposed to know.

Firstly, the courier who was to have delivered the message to the owner of the now 91—year old hotel handed the envelope wrongly to a tourist.

What happened was that the tourist was in the manager's office to complain about some letter he had not received. Just before the courier entered the manager's office, the manager decided to go to the loo and the tourist to use the telephone. So, there was this important looking gentleman holding the telephone when the courier came in. Thus, the mix—up compounded by the fact that the courier, in his hurry (he had to deliver 40 letters a clay,), handed over a hotel brochure which he should have brought to the DBS, his next place on the schedule.

Secondly. because, on reaching the DBS, he realised he had left the hotel brochure behind at Raffles Hotel, the courier then thought it better to sort things out before he went on his rounds the following day.

That day never did come. The courier was arrested for operating as a part time 4D runner. The DBS never got to know that Raffles Hotel was to be integrated into their development plans for the area.

But, au, you might ask, what about the Preservation of Monuments Board (PMB), the most important group?

The PMB? Qf course, it was the very first to know of the government 's decision.

But, because the letter which arrived at its office came on, of all days. April 1st, officials did not believe one word of it. They thought it was a particularly elaborate joke that some prankster had tried to play on them. So they passed the letter around and had a good chuckle. Preserving Raffles Hotel indeed, they said to one another.' On prime land? It was just too good to be true.

After all, the PMB has been fighting an almost impossible battle without much success.

In its years of existence, it has managed to "save just a few monuments" With no money, no community support and perhaps even no future in the great modernization rush, it has given up hope of such a coup as the salvation of Raffles Hotel.

Thus, when Minister Teh Cheang Wan made his announcement the other day, nearly everybody was surprised, most of all the PMB.

It is reliably learnt that they have been looking out every day now for that most important letter on the fate of Chinatown.

Well, Raffles has survived them all!

On March 4, 1987 Raffles was officially gazetted as a historical landmark under the Preservation of Monuments Board.

In 1988, the owners decided to invest $150 million in its restoration!

Announcing The Reopening Of Raffles

Raffles Hotel in 1907

On 16th September 1991
on Lee Kuan Yew's birthday
Raffles Hotel
reopened its doors

The Grand Old Lady Returns To Singapore

THE SUBTLE swish of overhead fans and the subdued chink of antique silver and china are back..Raffles Hotel, Singapore's "Grand Old Lady of the East" has staged her long-awaited comeback after a two-year restoration programme. Tourism's most talked-about dowager received her guests in style on September 16 when the all-suite hotel reopened its doors. It was a warm welcome, with all the hallmarks of understated elegance which earned Raffles Hotel its legendary name. The 104 suites with their lofty 14-foot high ceilings, grand arches, teak and marbled floors are now home to a new generation of travellers. The gardens which once provided a lush setting for writers such as Somerset Maugham have blossomed to now cover more than a quarter of the entire property.

The hotel's popular gift shop is now accompanied by a book gallery, provision shops, sundries shop and clothing shop - all offering tasteful memorabilia ranging from beautifully presented spices and preserves to stationery and toy tigers. The five Raffles shops are complemented by two specialty boutiques, Jim Thompson Thai Silk and the world-renowned New York jeweller, Tiffany and Co.

The "grand old lady" in the hotel itself is now joined by a well-bred retinue, housed in an adjoining complex which is simply called Raffles. Here the Raffles Hotel Museum and Gift Shop are housed, showcasing the hotel's early history. They are joined by a tempting collection of food and beverage outlets, including the famous Long Bar, home of the Singapore Sling. A Victorian-style Jubilee Hall and some 65 specialty shops all add to the sense of style for which the hotel is renowned.

Guests are treated to impeccable service as they alight from their vehicles in the circular driveway.

The centrepiece of the lobby is a large carpet hand-woven in the studio of the master carpet-maker, Saber, in Persia between 1930 and 1935.

...and dame of the East ...h her loyal subjects.

Left: French doors alongside the Tiffin Room open out to marble-floored corridors and leafy gardens.

Above: Comfortable cane armchairs beckon the weary traveller.

Left: Hard surfaced floors, teak furniture, oriental carpets, a piano and an antique Victrola are features of the Bar and Billiard Room.

A large expanse of greenery, with rows of palms and beautiful landscaping, sets the tropical mood in the Palm Court.

Left: Raffles memorabilia is available from the hotel shops - choose from stationery, miniature houses, silver jewellery or a set of placemats and coasters.

Above: A silk scarf with Noel Cowards autograph? A polo shirt or a golf cap?

Below: The speciality of the Tiffin Room is tiffin curry, which has been served in the main dining room since 1899.

Specially packaged spices, preserves, nuts, tea and coffee.

Memories Of Raffles
22 Years With a Grand Old Hotel
Roberto Pregarz

PATA GOLD AWARDS 1991, BALI
TOP HONOUR
"MEMORIES OF RAFFLES"

' ... This is a gem of a book, or rather a collection of gems whose setting is the heart of Singapore, Raffles Hotel - my Singapore and my Raffles in the good old days. Every page is a pleasure'
Dennis Bloodworth

'... A most interesting and delightful book and one which to all those who loved the Grand Old Layd must fill with nostalgia for the great days that are now, alas, gone!'
Russell Foreman

'... Fun and pain at the same time. The fun is reading the book. The pain? It makes you frightfully homesick to good old Raffles!'
Joplin Sinclair

'... Not only does it contain many of those legends and some notable recent events, but it "explains" one man's love and belief in the Raffles!'
Trevor J Hennigan

'... Droll, wistful, poignant, upbeat and often hilariously funny!'
Raymond Flower

'... A nice writing style - a great voice which hallmarks the book. I can hear Roberto telling these stories which is the exact effect required of a book of this nature!'
Goh Eck Kheng

'... It is so interesting to read the stories which then reminds me of events that took place during the seventies and eighties that shaped the course and indeed the survival of dear old Raffles!'
Colin Shaw

'... Roberto makes the most of his book and his experience with the same light-hearted abandon and concentration he brings to perfecting his hotels, in their historic setting.'
Gavin Young

ISTANA
SINGAPORE

19 May 1992

Mr Roberto Pregarz
General Manager
Executive Office
River View Hotel Singapore
382 Havelock Road
Singapore 0316

Dear Mr Pregarz

I have enjoyed reading your book "Memories of Raffles", especially so because the luminaries and journalists mentioned were known to me, some very closely. Wally Crouch, Ilsa Sharp and Bob Elegant are three of them from the Fourth Estate. I also know Tan Chin Tuan and Tresise fairly well. I also have some fond memories of Raffles, but nothing near what you had scintillatingly recorded in your book. When our paths cross again we may perhaps compare more notes.

Mrs Wee joins me in wishing you and your charming family all the very best.

Yours sincerely

WEE KIM WEE
PRESIDENT

President Wee Kim Wee recognises Raffles' contribution to the Nation's Charity chest.

84